A Book of
Orthodox Church
Terminology

Forward

Often times people are not familiar with various terms used within the Orthodox Church. This is true of long-time faithful and of inquirers and converts to the Church. In fact, there are many terms that we may think we know due to their use in modern Western Christendom but, in fact, the term is more nuanced or entirely different within Orthodoxy.

For this reason I have compiled the following common theological, liturgical and spiritual terms used in the Orthodox Church. This book can be used as an educational tool for catechetical purposes or as a simple reference guide for terms you may not be familiar with. It does not represent an encyclopedic description of each term but rather a simple definition to grasp a basic understanding. Where possible multiple languages are represented when common names are used in Greek or Slavic usages. This list is by no mean comprehensive but does include most terms used on a day-to-day basis in most parishes.

Priest Michael Lillie

AARON'S ROD. (an appellation of the Theotokos) Just as Aaron's Rod sprouted miraculously in the Old Testament, so too, the Theotokos has budded forth the Flower of Immortality, Christ our God (Num. 17:1-11)

ABBA The Aramaic term of intimacy used in addressing one's father, somewhat equivalent to the English "Daddy." Christ uses Abba in addressing God the Father. St. Paul tells believers that their relationship with God through the Holy Spirit is so personal that they too may speak to Him as intimately as to their own father (Mark 14:36; Rom. 8:15).

Abbess. (from masc. abbot; Gr. *Hegoumeni*). The female superior of a community of nuns, appointed by a bishop; Mother Superior. She has general authority over her community and nunnery under the supervision of a bishop.

Abbot. (from Aram. *abba*, father; Gr. *Hegoumenos*, Sl. *Nastoyatel*). The head of a monastic community or monastery, appointed by a bishop or elected by the members of the community. He has ordinary jurisdiction and authority over his monastery, serving in particular as spiritual father and guiding the members of his community.

ABORTION. The termination of a pregnancy by taking the life of the baby before it comes to full term. The Scriptures teach, "For You formed my inward parts; You covered me in my mother's womb" (Psalm 138[139]:13). When an unborn child is aborted, a human being is killed. For the Christian, all children, born or unborn, are precious in God's sight and a gift from Him and abortion is a mortal sin.

Absolution The prayer offered by a bishop or presbyter for the forgiveness of sins. Following His glorious Resurrection, Christ breathed on His Apostles and said, "Receive the Holy Spirit. If you forgive the sins of any, they are forgiven them; if you retain the sins of any, they are retained" John 20:22, 23). This gift of proclaiming God's forgiveness of sins remains forever in the Church. It is exercised in the sacraments of baptism and confession—the reconciliation to the Church of Christian believers who have sinned and repented. The priest or bishop is the witness who bears testimony to the repentance; only God forgives sins (see article, "Confession," at 1 John 1).

Abstinence. (Gr. *Nisteia*). A penitential practice consisting of voluntary deprivation of certain foods for religious reasons. In the Orthodox Church, days of abstinence are observed on Wednesdays and Fridays, or during other specific periods, such as the Great Lent (see fasting).

Acolyte. The follower of a priest; a person assisting the priest in church ceremonies or services. In the early Church, the acolytes were adults; today, however, the duties are performed by children (altar boys).

Advent A forty-day period of prayer, repentance, and fasting in preparation for Christmas. The word stems from the Latin word for "coming"; during the fast the faithful prepare for the coming of Christ at Christmas. See also *Nativity Fast* & *Abstinence*.

Aër. (Sl. *Vozdukh*). The largest of the three veils used for covering the paten and the chalice during or after the Eucharist. It represents the shroud of Christ. When the creed is read, the priest shakes it over the chalice, symbolizing the descent of the Holy Spirit.

AERIAL TOLL-HOUSES. The teaching of Aerial Toll-Houses regards the soul's journey after its departure from the body, and is related to the particular judgment. In its most general form, it refers to the idea that after death, the demons attempt to find a basis for taking the soul to Hades, while the angels and the prayers of the living defend the soul if it can be defended. Whether the soul is finally seized by the demons, or taken to heaven depends on the state of the soul at death. In either case, the soul then experiences a foretaste of what it can expect after the final judgment. Many have understood this to be an allegorical presentation of the particular judgment. See JUDGMENT & ALLEGORY.

Affinity. (Gr. *Syngeneia*). The spiritual relationship existing between an individual and his spouse's relatives, or, most especially, between godparents and godchildren. The Orthodox Church considers affinity an impediment to marriage.

AFTERFEAST An afterfeast (also known as postfeast) is a period of time following certain major feasts of the Christian year during which the feast continues to be celebrated. The liturgical life of the Church reflects this extended celebration by continuing to express the themes of the feast in the divine services celebrated during the afterfeast. Most commemorations that have an afterfeast also have a forefeast.

Agape. (Gr. "Love"). Feast of love; the common meal of fellowship eaten in gatherings of the early Christians (1 Cor. 11: 20-34). Agape is also the name of the Pascha Vespers Service held in the early afternoon on Pascha day. The faithful express their brotherly love and exchange the kiss of love honoring the resurrected Christ.

Age of Reason. This is the time in life when an individual begins to distinguish between right and wrong and becomes morally responsible for himself. It is considered to begin at the age of seven or so, and no later than twelve. Orthodox children will begin to confess their sins at this time.

Agnets. (see lamb).

AGNOSTICISM. The philosophical position that the existence or non-existence of God is unknowable. Condemned by the Orthodox Church for being a belief in error for denial of the truth of God and Jesus Christ.

Agrapha. (Gr. "verbal words; not written"). Sayings or deeds of Christ which were never written or recorded in the Gospels (cf. John 21:25).

Akathistos Hymn. 1)Originally a hymn of praise comprising twenty-four stanzas and sung at the Salutation Services, dedicated to Virgin Mary *Theotokos*. It is divided into four parts, one part sung on each Friday of the Great

Lent. On the fifth Friday, the entire set is sung in commemoration of a miracle performed by the Virgin in Constantinople (626 A.D.). The hymn is also known as "Salutations" (Gr. *Heretismoi*). 2) Further Akathist hymns have been written in praise to the Savior, the All-Holy Theotokos, or some Saint, which may be sung in church or at home.

Akriveia. Strictness, meaning strict adherence, precision, or exactness in application to Church canons. The opposite of oikonomia. See ECONOMY.

AKEDIA - (in Latin, accidie) is literally fatigue or exhaustion, but in technical usage refers to the spiritual and physical lethargy which can plague those pursuing the eremetic life. The reference in Psalm 90 (91 MT) to the "demon of noonday" is traditionally identified as akedia. It can take the form of listlessness, dispersion of thoughts, or being inattentively immersed in useless activity.

Alb. (Lat.; Gr. *stichari[on]*; Sl. *Podriznik*). The long white undergarment of the clergy, with close sleeves, worn under the chasuble (Phelonion) or the *sakkos*.

Allegory A story filled with symbolism illustrating a spiritual reality beyond the actual historical event being described. In the ancient Church, scholars of the School of Alexandria tended to consider many incidents in the Bible as allegorical, whereas the School of Antioch practiced a more historical approach to Scripture. Although Scripture contains some pure allegory (some parables of Christ, portions of Revelation), overemphasis on allegory may tend to de-emphasize or even deny the historicity of Holy Scripture. On the other hand, a denial of allegory robs the Scriptures of their deeper meaning. It is possible for a story to be both historical and allegorical. The majority of Church Fathers combined both elements in interpreting the Bible. See Luke 15:4-7; Gal. 4:21-26. See also TYPE.

Alleluia The Greek form of the Hebrew word Hallelujah, which means "praise God." Orthodox Christians sing a chorus of Alleluia interspersed with psalm verses prior to the Gospel reading at the Divine Liturgy.

All-Night Vigil. consists of a joining of Great Vespers and Matins and 1ˢᵗ hour into one Service. In ancient times and now in many monasteries, this service literally lasts all night (from early evening until daybreak of the following day), but in parish life, as well as certain cathedrals and monasteries, the All-Night Vigil may last for only two to four hours. See VIGIL

All-Saints Sunday. (Gr. *Agion Panton*). A feast day of the Orthodox Church collectively commemorating all the Saints of the church who have remained anonymous. This feast day is celebrated on the Sunday following Pentecost.

Alms. Works of mercy or monetary gifts given to help the poor. Throughout the Scriptures, God's people are called to help those less fortunate than themselves (see Matt. 25:31-46).

Alpha-Omega. The first and the last letters of the Greek alphabet, symbolizing "the beginning and the end," or the divinity and eternity of Christ (Rev. 1: 8). These two letters also form the monogram of Christ.

Altar. (Hebr. "a place of sacrifice"; Gr. *hieron*; Sl. *prestol*). In Orthodox architecture, the term signifies the area of the sanctuary divided from the rest of the church by the *iconostasis*.

Altar Boy. See ACOLYTE

Altar Bread. (see *Prosphoro*).

ALTAR CLOTHS - 1) *Gr. Katasaskion, SI. Sratchitsa*, a white cloth covering the whole altar table. It represents the Winding Sheet in which our Lord was wrapped for burial. 2) Sl. Inditia, a richly-embroidered cloth over the white cloth, representing Christ's Robe of Glory; 3) Sl. Iliton, the cloth in which the Antimension is wrapped.

Altar Table. (Gr. *Hagia Trapeza*; Sl. *Prestol*). The square table in the middle of the altar, made of wood or marble, on which the Eucharist is offered. It is dressed with the "Altar Cloth" and contains the relics deposited there by the consecrating bishop. The center of the table is occupied by the folded *Antiminsion,* on which the ceremonial gospel book is placed, and behind this is the tabernacle with the "reserved gifts."

Ambon. (Gr.; Sl. *Amvon,* "an elevated place, podium"). A small raised platform or elaborate podium at the left (north) side of the solea and in the front of the *iconostasis.* Decorated with representations of the four Evangelists, it is the place on which the deacon or priest reads the Gospel and delivers his sermon..

Amen. "So be it" in Hebrew. Amen is said or sung at the close of a prayer or hymn, showing the agreement of the people to what has been said (Deut. 27:15 26; 1 Cor. 14:16).

Amnos. (see lamb).

ANABATHMOI -'Hymns of Ascent'. These hymns are based on Ps. 120-134 and refer to the Church's ascension to heaven. They are sung in Matins preceding the Prokeimenon and Gospel.

Analogion. (Gr. Sl. *analoy*). A wooden stand or podium usually with a sloped top, it is used as a stand for the gospel book or an icon.

Anathema. (Gr. "a curse, suspension"). The spiritual suspension with which the church may expel a person from his or her community for various reasons, especially denial of the faith or other mortal sins. The church also may proclaim an anathema against the enemies of the faith, such as heretics and traitors, in a special service conducted on the Sunday of Orthodoxy (first Sunday of Lent).

Ancestral Sin – see ORINGINAL SIN

Anchorite. (Gr. *Anachoritis,* "a departurer"). A solitary monk or hermit; an individual who withdraws from society and lives a solitary life of silence and prayer.

Angels. (Gr. *Angelos*, "messenger"). Bodiless beings, purely spirits, created by God before man. They are superior in nature and intelligence to man; and, like man, they have understanding and free will. Some of them are appointed to guard the faithful (guardian angels). Angels are grouped in nine orders (*tagmata*) as follows: Angels; Archangels; Principalities; Powers; Virtues; Dominions; Thrones; Cherubim; Seraphim. In the Orthodox worship, every Monday is dedicated to the angels.

Annunciation. (Gr. *Evangelismos*). A feast of the Orthodox Church (March 25) commemorating the visit of Archangel Gabriel to the Virgin Mary to "announce" that she was chosen to be the Mother of God (Luke 1: 26-33).

Anteri. (see cassock).

Antichrist. Literally, "against Christ" or "instead of Christ." Antichrist is used by John to refer to (a) the opponent of Christ who will arise at the end of this age, and (b) the "many antichrists" who stand against the Son of God (1 John 2:18, 22; 4:3).

Antidoron. (Gr. "instead of the gift"). A small piece of the altar bread (*prosphoron*) given to each of the faithful after the celebration of the Eucharist. Originally it was given to those who could not take communion, but it became a practice for it to be offered to all the faithful.

Antimens or Antiminsion. (Gr. and Lat. compounds, "in place of a table"; Sl. *Antimins*). It is a rectangular piece of cloth, of linen or silk, with representations of the entombment of Christ, of the four Evangelists, and with scriptural passages related to the Eucharist. The *antimens* must be consecrated by the head of the church (a Patriarch or Archbishop) and must always lie on the Altar Table. No sacrament, especially the Divine Liturgy, can be performed without a consecrated *antimens*.

Antiphon. (Gr. "alternate utterance or chanting").

1.A short verse from the scriptures, especially the psalms, sung or recited during the liturgy and other church services. In Slavic usage the first three hymns sung at the Divine Liturgy (Ps. 103; Ps. 146 and Only-begotten Son... the Beatitudes)

2.Any verse or hymn sung recited by one part of the choir or chanters in response to another part. Hence this type of singing in steps is called antiphonal.

APOKATASTSIS – The name of a heresy saying that all will be saved, even if they reject God. In 543 the doctrine of apokatastasis was condemned by the Synod of Constantinople.

Apostol. This contains the readings from the Acts of the Apostles and the Epistles for the whole year i.e., the entire New Testament outside of the Gospels and the Apocalypse (Revelation) of St. John. It too is divided into pericopes and also includes the Prokeimena and Alleluia verses which precede and follow the Epistle readings. See Prokeimen & Alleluia

Apocrypha. (Gr. "hidden or secret"). Some of the books of the Bible not accepted by all denominations of Christians as true and divinely inspired. Some of them were written much later but attributed to important individuals of the apostolic times, thus bearing a misleading title (*pseudepigrapha*).

Apodosis. (Gr., Sl. *Otdanive*). Leave-taking. The "octave-day" of a feast day which lasts more than one day and usually occurs eight days after the actual feast day. i.e. The *Apodosis* of Pascha occurs forty days after the feast, on the eve of the Ascension.

Apologetics. (Gr. "defenders").

1.The individuals and saints who defended the faith and the Church by their ability to present, explain, and justify their faith.

2.The theological science and art of presenting, explaining, and justifying the reasonableness of the Christian faith.

Apolytikion. (Gr. "dismissal"). The dismissal hymn sung in honor of a saint, Christ, or the Virgin Mary on the occasion of their feast day, especially at the end of the Vespers Service. See TROPARION.

Apostasy. Literally, "turning away." This sin is committed when a Christian or body of believers rejects the true faith of Christ (1 Tim. 1:5 7; 4:1-3).

Apostikha. These are Stikhera accompanied by verses usually taken from the Psalms. The Apostikha is found at the end of Vespers and also at the end of Matins on ordinary weekdays.

Apostle. Literally, "one who is sent." Apostle is used as a title for the Twelve Disciples who formed the foundation of the NT Church, replacing, symbolically, the twelve tribes of Israel. In order to maintain this symbolism, Matthias was elected to replace Judas (Acts 1:15 26). The word is also used of the Seventy (or 72) sent by Christ, as well as of Paul, the repentant persecutor whom the risen Jesus sent as "apostle to the Gentiles" (Rom. 11:13). Great missionaries in the Church, such as Mary Magdalene (the "apostle to the apostles"), Thekla, Nina, Vladimir, and Innocent of Alaska are called "equal to the apostles." The extension of the apostolic ministry in the Church today is in the episcopacy. See also EPISCOPACY.

Apostolic Canons. A collection of eighty-five decrees of ecclesiastical importance, referring mainly to ordination and the discipline of the clergy. The church believes that they were originally written by the Apostolic fathers.

Apostolic Fathers. Men who lived during the first century of Christianity; for the most part, this group comprised the disciples of the Apostles; their teachings and writings are of great spiritual value to Christians. Major fathers are St. Ignatius of Antioch, St. Polycarp of Smyrna, St. Clement of Rome, and the unknown author of Didache.

Apostolic Succession. The direct, continuous, and unbroken line of succession transmitted to the bishops of the Church by the Apostles. The bishops, who form a collective body (that is the leadership of the Church), are considered to be successors of the Apostles, and, consequently, the duties and powers given to the Apostles by Christ are transmitted through "the laying-on-of-hands" to the bishops and priests who succeeded them by ordination (*cheirotonia*) to priesthood. Succession includes not just apostolic ordination, but also, Orthodox doctrine and full communion from the Apostles to the current episcopacy of the Orthodox Church. All three elements are constitutive of apostolic succession.

Archangels. An Angelic order of angels of higher rank. The names of two archangels, Michael and Gabriel, are known (feast day on November 8); they are also known as "leaders of the angelic armies" (*taxiarchai*).

Archbishop. A head bishop. The second award of Bishops in the Russian/Slavic usage (see also Metropolitan).

Archdeacon. A senior deacon, usually a monastic or one that is serving with a bishop of higher rank (Archbishop or Patriarch).

Archdiocese. An ecclesiastical jurisdiction, usually a metropolis headed by an Archbishop.

Archimandrite. (Gr. "head of the flock or cloister"). A celibate presbyter of high rank assisting the bishop or appointed abbot in a monastery. In the Russian tradition, some Archimandrites have the right to wear the mitre and the mantle (*mitrophoros*).

ARIANISM - The name of a heresy saying which denied the true Divinity of Jesus Christ, so-called after its author, Arius, a presbyter in the Church of Alexandria. This heresy was condemned at the first Ecumenical Council held in Nicea in 325.

ARK – 1) Reference to the Ark of the Covenant, a created receptacle in the Jewish Temple which somehow contained the uncontainable God. 2) (an appellation of the Theotokos) The Theotokos is often called an Ark, for the Glory of God settled on her, just as the Glory of God descended on the

Mercy Seat of the Old Testament Ark of the Covenant (Ex. 25:10-22).

Armenian Church. A monophysite denomination which broke from the Orthodox Church in the fifth century (451 A.D.). See MONOPHYSITE

Artoklasia. (see Vespers & Artos).

Artophorion. literally "the box of the holy Communion,". It is also calleda "Pyx" or "Ciborium," or the Box of the holy Communion," enclosing the Holy Communion, to be given to the sick and prisoners. See PYX

Artos. (Greek: Ἄρτος, "leavened loaf", "bread") is a loaf of leavened bread that is blessed during services. A large Artos is baked with a seal depicting the resurrection for use at Pascha. Smaller loaves are blessed during great vespers in a ritual called Artoklasia and in other occasions like feast days, weddings, memorial services etc.

Ascension. The ascent of Christ to Heaven following His Resurrection as Son of God in the flesh (Luke 24:50, 51; Acts 1:9-11). Christ's Ascension completes the union of God and humanity, for a Man who is God now reigns in Heaven. A movable feast day, forty days after Pascha.

Ascetic. (Gr. "one who practices [spiritual] exercises"). A monk who has accepted a monastic life and intensively practices self discipline, meditation, and self-denial, motivated by love of God.

Asceticism. (from Gr. askesis, "athlete") A life of struggle —the crucifixion of the desires of the flesh, through a life of prayer, fasting, and self-denial. Through asceticism the Christian fights temptation to sin and thereby grows in spiritual strength. Such spiritual classics as The Philokalia and The Ladder of Divine Ascent give directions for the ascetic life (see Luke 9:23; Gal. 5:24).

Ascetic Theology. A theological field studying the teachings and the writings of the ascetics of the Church (see also mysticism).

Assumption or Dormition. Name given to the Assumption of the Mother of God, derived from the Latin word dormire, to sleep. Literally it is "sleeping," in Slavonic "Ouspeniye." The feast of the Dormition or Falling-asleep of the Theotokos is celebrated on the 15th of August, preceded by a two-week fast. This feast, which is also sometimes called the Assumption, commemorates the death, resurrection and glorification of Christ's mother. It proclaims that Mary has been **"assumed"** by God into the heavenly kingdom of Christ in the fullness of her spiritual and bodily existence.

Asterisk. (Gr. "little star"; Sl. *Zvezditsa*). A sacred vessel having two arched metal bands held together in such a fashion as to form the shape of a cross. It is placed on the paten and serves to prevent the veil from touching the particles of the Eucharist.

Atheism. (Gr. "godlessness"). Denial of the existence of God. An atheist accepts only the material and physical world or what can be proven by reason.

Authority. The rule of God over the world and the legitimate authority given by God to those ordained to shepherd the faithful (Heb. 13:17). Also, one of the nine choirs of angels. See also ANGELS.

Atonement. (Gr. *exilasmos*). The redemptive activity of Christ in reconciling man to God. The Orthodox believe that Christ, through His death upon the cross, atoned or paid for human sins.

ATTRIBUTES OF GOD - The powers and virtues that make God what He is - Almighty, Eternal, Omniscient, Omnipresent, Merciful, Just. Also, He is - ineffable, inconceivable, invisible, incomprehensible, ever-existing and eternally the same

Autocephalous. (Gr. "appointing its own leader"). The status of an Orthodox church which is self-governed and also has the authority to elect or appoint its own leader or head (*cephale*) though remaining in spiritual communion with the body of the greater Orthodox Church.

Autonomy. (Gr. "self-rule"). The status of an Orthodox Church that is self-ruled without severing ties with the Mother Church. An autonomous church is governed by its prelate, who is chosen by a superior jurisdiction, usually by a patriarchate.

Axios. (Gr. "worthy"). An exclamation made at ordination to signify the worthiness of the individual chosen to become a clergyman.

-B-

BALDACHIN. A canopy over the altar, usually supported on pillars. Not a common today in the church.

BANNERS. Metallic or of brocaded cloth with sacred icons, attached to poles, carried at the head of processions.

Baptism. (Gr. "immersion into water for purification"). A sacrament instituted by Christ Himself, baptism is the regeneration effected by means "of water and the spirit" (John 3:5). An Orthodox baptism is administered by the priest (in case of absolute emergency, however, by a layman (*aerobaptismos*)) through three complete immersions and by pronouncing the individual's name along with the name of the Trinity, "the Father and the Son and the Holy Spirit. Amen." Chrismation follows immediately after baptism.

Baptismal Font. (Gr. *Kolymbethra*). A large, often movable, circular basin on a stand, containing the water for immersion in Baptism. It symbolizes the Jordan River or the pool of Siloam.

Baptismal Garments. (Gr. *Fotikia* or *baptisika*; Sl. *krizhma*). The The white garments brought by the godparent to dress the infant immediately after the immersion in Baptism. In Orthodoxy, these garments are considered sacred and must be either kept safely or destroyed by fire.

Baptismal Name. (Gr. *onoma*). The individual's name given in baptism, commonly the name of a saint who becomes the individual's Patron Saint. In Greek custom the baptismal names of the first-born are usually those of their grandparents. In other traditions it is a common custom to receive the name of the saint on whose day one was born.

Baptistry. A special room or area in the form of a pool for baptizing in the ancient Church. Gradually, it was replaced by the baptismal font (see *baptismal font*).

Beatitudes. (Gr. *Makarismoi*).

1.Blessings promised to individuals for various reasons.

2.The eight blessings given by Christ during his Sermon on the Mount (Matt. 5: 3-12).

3.Salutation addressed to some Orthodox Patriarchs or Metropolitans ("Your Beatitude").

BEGOTTEN. In the creed, the phrase, "Begotten not made" is said to contradict the false doctrine of Arius who impiously taught that the Son of God was made. See ARIANISM & CREED.

Belief. The acceptance of the truths of the gospel. More than a mental assent, belief as used in the NT includes trusting in God from the heart. Such belief results from (1) hearing the Word of God (Rom. 10:17) and (2) a gift of the Holy Spirit (Eph. 2:8). Although a Christian is saved by belief in Christ, faith without action (that is, a distinct movement of the will to follow Christ) is hollow and void of the righteousness necessary to salvation.

BELLS. The ringing of bells serves two functions in the Orthodox Church. The first is for calling the faithful to divine services, and the second is to announce the beginning of various parts of the services to those faithful who are absent from the church.

BEMA - the raised floor or platform in the Paschan end of Orthodox churches upon which the altar, with the altar table, is located. The word bema comes from the Greek, meaning a platform, step, tribunal, or judgment seat. In general, the platform extends into the nave from the sanctuary and is separated by an iconostasis. The area in the nave is called the *solea* with the *ambon*.

Benediction. (Lat. "blessings to glorify God"). The closing blessing offered by a clergyman at the end of a service or other activity.

BETROTHAL. (Sl. Obrucheniye) The first part of the Rite of Matrimony in which a formal and binding promise of marriage is made and rings are placed on the fingers of the bride and groom. See MARRIAGE.

BIBLE is the divinely inspired Word of God *(II Timothy 3:16),* and is a crucial part of God's self-revelation to the human race. The Old Testament tells the history of that revelation from Creation through the Age of the Prophets. The New Testament records the birth and life of Jesus as well as the writings of His Apostles. It also includes some of the history of the early Church and especially sets forth the Church's apostolic doctrine. Though these writings were read in the Churches from the time they first appeared, the earliest listings of all the New Testament books exactly as we know them today, is found in the 33rd Canon of a local council held at Carthage in 318, and in a fragment of St. Athanasius of Alexandria's Festal Letter in 367. Both sources list all of the books of the New Testament without exception. A local council, probably held at Rome in 382, set forth a complete list of the canonical books of both the Old and New Testaments. The Scriptures are at the very heart of Orthodox worship and devotion.

BIER. This is the structure that houses the Epitaphion following the procession of Holy Friday Vespers, and is used to carry it in the procession of Holy Saturday Matins that evening. See EPITAPHION.

Bishop. (Gr. *Episkopos, Archiereas*).Literally, Overseer. A clergyman who has received the highest of the sacred orders. A bishop is the leader of a local community of Christians. In the New Testament there is no clear distinction between the offices of bishop and elder (presbyter), both of which function as leaders of the community. However, by the mid- to late first century, the Church began to reserve the title bishop for the men of spiritual qualification who were consecrated to follow the Apostles in their office of oversight. A bishop must be ordained by at least three other bishops and is considered a successor of the Apostles.

BLAGOVEST - *The Announcement.* This is a slow rhythmic, unhurried striking of one bell, which is usually rung for the announcing of the beginning of services.

Blasphemy. Evil and reproachful language directed at God, the Virgin, the Saints, or sacred objects. Blasphemy against the Holy Spirit is a mortal and unforgivable sin because it presumes that God's saving action in this particular case is impossible (cf. Matt. 12: 31).

BLESSING - A ceremony or rite by which the Church dedicates persons, places or things to a sacred purpose, or attaches to them a spiritual value. Places that are blessed - a church, cemetery, house; things - water (on the Feast of the Baptism of our Lord), vestments, icons, food on Pascha Day.

Book of Gospels. This book contains the text of the four Gospels (Matthew, Mark, Luke and John) arranged in sections called pericopes (or zachalo in Russian). This book normally rests on the Holy Table, and is customarily treated in the same way as the Holy Icons, itself being regarded as an Icon of the Savior in His teaching ministry. See GOSPEL

Book of Epistles. See APOSTOL

Book of Needs. (Russian Trebnik). This book contains five of the Sacraments (the Divine Liturgy and Holy Orders are omitted), the Funeral Service, and various other services commonly used.

Born Again. Literally, "born from above." A person must be born again to new life in Christ to enter God's eternal Kingdom. This new birth takes place through the sacrament of Holy Baptism John 3:16; Rom. 6:3, 4; Gal. 3:27). Spiritual life begins by receiving the Holy Spirit in baptism, and it is a dynamic process which continues throughout life.

BOWING - Besides kneeling and standing, bowing by a simple inclination of the head is a manner of expressing reverence and respect in the church. Bowing is appropriate after making the sign of the cross, when receiving blessing from the priest, on entering and leaving the church and when passing in front of the altar.

Branch Theory. is a belief, outside of Orthodoxy, that communities of Christians that are not in communion with each other, may still be a branch of the One Church. Recently this has been expressed as a two lung theory by Roman Catholic writers, or there being three main branches by Anglican writers. Sometimes, by others, the entire "tree" is called an invisible church. Branch Theory implies that many, if not all, Christians communities can trace their history, through other "branches of Christianity" back to the Apostolic Church. The Orthodox Church believes that more is necessary to claim apostolic succession. The community needs to hold the apostolic teachings, and be as one with all who hold the faith. To choose to hold other beliefs is heresy. The Orthodox Church rejects such a proposition and sees the Orthodoxy as the ONE visible Church in which all others have fallen away. See ECUMENISM & APOSTOLIC SUCCESSION.

BRIDEGROOM - (an appellation or Title of Jesus) " And Jesus said unto them, Can the children of the bride chamber mourn, as long as the bridegroom is with them? but the days will come, when the bridegroom shall be taken from them, and then shall they fast." Matt 9:15

BRIGHT WEEK - Every day during the week of Pascha, called Bright Week by the Church, the paschal services are celebrated in all their splendor. The Pascha baptismal procession is repeated daily. The royal doors of the sanctuary remain open. The joy of the Resurrection and the gift of the Kingdom of eternal life continue to abound. Then, at the end of the week, on Saturday evening, the second Sunday after Pascha is celebrated in remembrance of the appearance of Christ to the Apostle Thomas "after eight days" (Jn 20:26).

Brothers of the Lord. St. James, the first bishop of Jerusalem, Joses, Simon, and Judas are referred to as brothers of Christ (Matt. 13:55). In the ancient Middle East one's close relatives were frequently referred to as brothers and sisters. Also, there is an ancient tradition that the "brothers and sisters" of Christ were actually children of St. Joseph from an earlier marriage; they are called the children of Mary although they are actually her stepchildren. Thus, these references to siblings of Christ do not contradict the ancient belief of the Orthodox Church that the Virgin Mary was a virgin before, during, and after the birth of Christ. The absence of blood brothers is suggested by Christ's act of entrusting Mary to the care of the apostle John (John 19:26, 27), which would have been against the Mosaic Law had she had other natural children.

Burial. (Gr. *Taphe*; Sl. *Pogrebeniye*). The act of interment of the dead body of one of the faithful in consecrated ground, according to the appropriate Orthodox rites and service of burial (*Nekrosimos*). The Church may deny an Orthodox burial to those who have committed a mortal sin such as blasphemy, suicide, denial of faith, or acceptance of cremation.

BURNING BUSH - (an appellation of the Theotokos) On Mt. Sinai, Moses saw the Bush that was burning, but was not consumed. So too, the Theotokos bore the fire of Divinity, but was not consumed (Ex. 3:1-6).

Byzantine. Referring or attributed to Byzantium, the ancient Greek city on the Bosporus, which later (331 A.D.) became the capital of the Paschan Roman Empire, and then of the Medieval Greek Empire of Constantinople. Its people are known as Byzantines and its cultural heritage as Byzantine (i.e., Byzantine art, Empire, church, architecture, music, etc.).

Byzantine rite.

1.Performing church services according to the Paschan Orthodox tradition.

2. Uniats Christians are called the Roman Catholics of the Byzantine Rite because while accepting the Roman Catholic dogmas and recognizing the supremacy of the Pope, they hold to the services and the customs of the Orthodox Church. They celebrate the Divine Liturgy in the Slavonic, or other native language.

BYZANTINE STYLE - The manner of church building and decoration of Greek or Russian origin. The model is the church of the Holy Wisdon (Hagia Sophia) in Constantinople, consecrated in 562. Many Western churches have been patterned after the Byzantine Style.

-C-

Calendar. (Gr. *Hemerologion*). The yearly system determining the Orthodox holidays and hours. The Orthodox year begins on September 1. Because all feasts were arranged according to the ***Julian (old)*** Calendar, many Orthodox churches follow it to the present day, while other Orthodox churches have adopted the ***Gregorian (new)*** Calendar (since 1924).

Candles. (Gr. *Keri[on]*). Candles made of beeswax are used in the Orthodox Church as a form of sacrifice, devotion, & offering to God or Saints. They are used in various Orthodox services and ceremonies and are symbolic of Christ, who is "the Light of the World." According to a different symbolism, the two elements of a candle represent the two natures of Christ: the Divine (the burning wick) and the Human (the wax body).

Canon. (Gr. "rule, measure, standard").

1.The Canon of the scriptures or the official list of books recognized by the church as genuine and inspired by God.

2.The Canon of Matins (a collection of hymns consisting of nine odes, the Heirmos, and sung at the Matins Service, the Orthros).

3.The Liturgical Canon, which refers to all liturgical material, including the Creed, used for the Liturgy and the consecration of the Eucharist (see also *kanon* and *Typikon*).

Canonization. The official declaration by the Church that a deceased Christian of attested virtue is a saint, to be honored as such, and worthy of imitation by the faithful.

Canons. - Literally, "a rule. (Gr)" It describes (1) the inspired Books of the Bible - the Canon of Scripture; (2) the rules and decrees issued by the early Church (Acts 15:23-29) and by Ecumenical Councils - Canon Law; and (3) certain parts of worship, such as the Liturgical Canon or the Canon of Matins. A lengthy hymn composed of nine Odes, with each Ode being made up of the Irmos, Troparion, Theotokion and Katabasia. It is a basic element of Matins and may also appear elsewhere.

CANTOR (or Lector) - A layman who sings or leads the congregation in singing the responses at services. He also reads the Epistle.

Capital Sin (or Mortal or Deadly sin). Great offenses against God, or moral faults which, if habitual, could result in the spiritual death of the individual. The following sins are considered to be mortal: pride, covetousness, lust, anger, gluttony, envy, and sloth. These are the "Seven Deadly Sins" of the phrase.

Cassock. (Gr. *Anteri*; Sl. *Podrasnik*) is worn under the cassock. It symbolizes the death of a clergyman to this world and his burial and subsequent dedication to God and his heavenly kingdom.

(Gr. *Raso*; Sl. *ryassa*). The long black garment with large sleeves worn by the Orthodox clergy as their distinct attire. Another such cassock with narrow sleeves.

CATACOMBS - Catacomb (from the Greek kata kumbas, meaning "near the low place or ravine") was originally the name of a particular district in Rome, but later referred to subterranean Christian burial places throughout the Roman Empire.

Catechism. A summary of doctrine and instruction, teaching the Orthodox faith in the form of questions and answers. The catechetical or Sunday school of each parish is responsible for such instruction of children or other faithful.

Catechumen. (Gr. "those who learn the faith"). A convert to Christianity in the early church who received instruction in Christianity but was not yet baptized. Catechumens were permitted to attend the first part of the Eucharist (Liturgy of the Catechumens), but were dismissed before the Consecration of the Gifts.

CATHEDRA - (a) An elevated place in the center of the church where a bishop is robed and where he remains until the Little Entrance. (b) The chair for the sole use of the bishop in the sanctuary. It is a sign of the bishop's authority.

Cathedral. (Gr. "the main chair"). The principal church of a bishop's jurisdiction, the chief church in every diocese.

Catholic. (Gr. "universal, concerning the whole"; Sl. *Sobomaya*). A term describing the universality of the Christian message, claimed to be exclusively theirs by the Orthodox Church. The Orthodox Church calls all to accept the faith, which lacks nothing for man's salvific union with

God. However, in the West, it has come to mean the Roman Catholic church (v. Paschan Orthodox Church).

CELEBRANT - Person who celebrates the Holy Eucharist - priest or bishop. A deacon may not celebrate the Holy Eucharist, but may assist.

Celibacy. The unmarried state of life. Unlike the Roman Church, Orthodoxy permits a clergyman to be married; however, his marriage must occur before his ordination to be a deacon or presbyter. Orthodox bishops are only chosen from the celibate clergy, but widowers, who have accepted monastic vows, may also be chosen.

Censer. (Gr. *Thymiato*; Sl. *kadillo*).CENSER - Vessel with cover hung on chains used for burning incense in church ceremonies.

Chalice. (Gr. *Potirion*; Sl. *Vozduh*). A large cup of silver or gold, with a long-stemmed base, used for the Eucharist. It is one of the most sacred vessels of the church and is handled only by the clergy.

Chant. (Gr. *echos*; Sl. *glas*). The music proper to the Orthodox services. There are eight tones or modes in the Orthodox Byzantine chant, chanted by the chanters or cantors.

Chanter. (Gr. *Psaltis*). A lay person who assists the priest by chanting the responses and hymns in the services or sacraments of the church. Today, chanters have been replaced to some extent by choirs.

Chapel. (Gr. *Parekklisi[on]*; Sl. *Chasovnya*). A side altar attached to a larger church or a small building or room built exclusively or arranged for the worship of God. A chapel can belong to an individual or an institution, or can be part of a parish church.

CHARITY - In Christian theology charity, or love (agape), means an unlimited loving-kindness toward all others. We find the elements of the doctrine of charity in the Ten Commandments of the Law of God. (The term should not be confused with the more restricted modern use of the word charity to mean benevolent giving) see AGAPE.

Chasuble. (Gr. *feloni[on]*; Sl. *felon*). A sleeveless garment worn by the *presbyter* in the celebration of the liturgy. Short in front, with an elongated back, and an opening for the head, it is one of the most ancient vestments of the Church, symbolizing the seamless coat of Christ.

Chatjis. (see *Hatjis*).

Cherubic Hymn. (Gr. "the song of the angels"). Liturgical hymn sung after the Gospel-reading and during the Great Entrance. Its text in English is as follows: *"We, who mystically represent the Cherubim, And chant the thrice-holy hymn to the Life-giving Trinity, Let us set aside the cares of life That we may receive the King of all, Who comes invisibly escorted by the Divine Hosts."*

CHERUBIM - An order of angels near to the throne of God. St. Gregory the Great says the word means "'fulness of knowledge,' and they are so called because they are filled with a knowledge which is more perfect since they are allowed to behold the glory of God more closely." They kept the gates of Paradise after the Fall (Gen. 3:24).

CHILIASM – The name of a heresy saying that Christ will reign for a literal 1,000 years after the Second Coming.

Chrism. (Gr. *Myrron*). Sanctified oil composed of several ingredients and fragrances, used in the sacrament of Chrismation (after Baptism). The Holy Chrism in the Orthodox Church is exclusively prepared by the the head of Autocephalous Churches and is blessed in a series of preparations and ceremonies. Holy Thursday is customarily the day of its consecration.

Chrismation. The sacrament completing baptism, whereby one receives the gift of the Holy Spirit through anointing with the Chrism, a specially prepared oil which must be consecrated by a bishop. On several occasions in Acts, a baptized Christian received the gift of the Holy Spirit through the laying on of the hands of an Apostle (see Acts

8:14-17; 19:6). Chrismation is a continuation of that ancient practice in the Church in Acts 2. The Sacrament brings the seal and gift of the Holy Spirit and gives power to live the life of Christ.

Chrisom. (Gr. *Ladopano*; Sl. *knzhma*). A piece of white linen for the wrapping of the infant after Baptism. The Orthodox preserve it as a sacred object because it signifies the purity and holiness of the baptized Christian.

CHRIST - (Gr. the 'Annointed One') Jesus Christ, the Son of God, the second Person of the Holy Trinity, who was incarnate and became Man, and was crucified and on the third day He rose from the dead. By His death on the Cross he reconciled man with God and opened the way to eternal life to everyone who rightly believes in Him. (See: JESUS CHRIST)

CHRISTIAN - One who is baptized in the name of the Father, and of the Son, and of the Holy Ghost, and becomes a part of the Mystical Body of Christ which is His Church. Followers of Christ were first called Christians at Antioch (Acts 11:26). In modern times the name Christian has usually been claimed by every form of belief stemming from historic Christianity.

Christology. A subject or field of dogmatic theology examining the belief of the church and the history of beliefs about Christ.

Churching. (Gr. *Sarantismos*). A service of thanksgiving and blessing of women after childbirth. In the Orthodox church, this rite is performed on the fortieth day after birth and is reminiscent of the Old Testament ceremony of purification (Lev. 12: 2-8) and the presentation of Jesus at the Temple (Luke 2: 22-29).

CHURCH MILITANT - A term for members of the Church on earth in warfare against sin and evil, as distinguished from the members of the Church Triumphant in Heaven. (HEB. 12:23) Not that there are two churches, we believe in only One Holy Catholic and

Apostolic Church, all members of the One Church remain united to each other, and support each other in prayer.

CHURCH TRIUMPHANT - A term for members of the Church, the saints who have departed this life, as distinguished from the members of the Church Militant on earth, still in warfare against sin and evil. (HEB. 12:23) Not that there are two churches, we believe in only One Holy Catholic and Apostolic Church, all members of the One Church remain united to each other, and support each other in prayer. One can get a taste of the Church Triumphant here and now, in the participation in the Kingdom of Heaven at each Divine Liturgy service.

CIVIL MARRIAGE - Marriage contracted by civil authorities, like a Justice of the Peace. In the case of Orthodox faithful such marriage is not recognized as valid in the eyes of the Church. Marriage is a Holy Sacrament and must be solemnized by the Church.

Commandment. The Law of God, given first in the Ten Commandments on Mt. Sinai, and completed or fulfilled by the teaching of Christ (Ex. 20:1-17; Matt. 5:1—7:27; John 15:12).

Communion. (Gr. *koinonia*). A common union of the most intimate kind, enjoyed by Christians with God and with each other in the Church. This communion is especially realized in the mystery of the Holy Eucharist John 6:56; 1 Cor. 10:16, 17).The receiving of the sacrament of the Eucharist after proper preparation, fasting, and confession. Orthodox Christians are encouraged to receive communion as often as possible, even daily.

Communion of Saints. The Orthodox Church believes that all the people of God-members of the Church, either the living on earth or the departed in heaven-are in constant communion and fellowship with each other in faith, grace, and prayers, since they constitute one Body in Christ-the Church.

COMMUNION OF THE SICK - A special rite by which Holy Communion is taken to the sick. The Reserved Holy Gifts are kept in the Tabernacle on the Altar for this purpose. The Reserved Gifts are prepared by the priest on Holy Thursday. The communion of the sick is administered with preparatory prayers and confession.

Compline. (Gr. *Apodeipnon*; Sl. *Velikoye PovecheAye*). A worship service performed after dusk. It is often combined with Vespers to form the Evening service. There is a Great Compline and its abridgement, known as Small Compline.

CONCELEBRATION. The celebration of the Divine Liturgy by several priests at one altar at the same time, when one priest assists another in serving or celebrating the sacraments. The term is also used for bishops also.

Confession. (Gr. *Exomologisis*). The act of confessing or acknowledgment of sins by an individual before God in the presence of a priest, who serves as a spiritual guide and confessor (*pneumatikos*) authorized to ask for forgiveness and to administer a penance. Reference 1 John; John 20:22, 23; 1 John 1:9

Confessor.

1.*Pneumatikos* (see confession).

2.A person who defended and publicly confessed the Faith, thereby exposing himself to persecution (*Homologetis*).

CONFIRMATION - see Chrismation

Consecration. (Gr. *Heirotonia*). The ordination of an individual to priesthood through the sacrament of Holy Orders. See *Ordination*.

CONTRITION - Grieving over sins with determination to avoid them in the future.

Conversion The beginning of salvation, occurring when a person repents, believes the gospel, and enters into a personal relationship with Christ. Conversion is not merely a change of belief but the beginning of a new life in Christ (2 Cor. 5:17), which is a process of growth into the image and likeness of God. Our salvation is the working together of conversion, justification, and sanctification throughout life.

CONVERT - Any person who has reached the age of reason, not baptized or baptized outside of the Orthodox Church, renounces his errors and accepts the teachings of the Orthodox Church, is received as a member by Baptism, or by Chrismation, or Confession and Communion, as the case may require.

Corruption. The state of mortality and sinfulness, the universal condition of fallen humanity. All are born into a world suffering the consequences of the Fall, the sin of Adam and Eve. These consequences include physical suffering, death, lack of perfection and a tendency to sin. See Ps. 53:3; Is. 53:6; Rom. 3:23; 1 John 5:19. See Original Sin.

Cosmos. The universe, or "world," created by God from nothing. It is controlled by God; He is the life of the world. Sin has corrupted the entire cosmos, and the rule of evil will not be abolished until the Second Coming of Jesus Christ. The universe will finally be redeemed by Christ when He comes again to transform the cosmos into a new heaven and a new earth. See Gen. 1:1; Rom. 8:19-22; Rev. 21:1.

Consecration of a Church. (see *Engainia*).

Council, Ecumenical. (Gr. *Synodos*; Sl. *Sobor*). Assembly of representatives from all church jurisdictions convoked for the settlement of ecclesiastical or doctrinal problems and disputes. The Orthodox Church recognizes the following seven Ecumenical Councils:

1.*Nicaea*, in 325. Fathers present, 318. Condemned Arianism, defined divinity of Christ, and composed first part of Creed.

2.*Constantinople*, 381. Fathers, 180. Condemned Apollinarianism, defined divinity of the Holy Spirit, and completed the Creed.

3.*Ephesus*, 431. Fathers, 200. Condemned Nestorianism and defined the term Theotokos.

4.*Chalcedon*, 451. Fathers, 630. Condemned Monophysitism.

5.*Constantinople*, 553. Fathers, 165. Condemned heretics and pagans.

6.*Constantinople*, 680. Fathers, 281. Condemned Monothelitism. The so-called Quinisext or in Trullo was held in Constantinople.

7.*Constantinople* (Trullo), 692. Regulated disciplinary matters to complete the Fifth and the Sixth Ecumenical Councils.

8.*Nicaea*, 787 (again in 843). Fathers, 350. Condemned Iconoclasm.

Covenant. An agreement or testament between men or between God and His people. In the Old Testament, God chose the people of Israel, ending with John the Baptist, to prepare the way for the coming of His Only Begotten Son. Through Christ, the covenant was perfected, and the promises of God to Abraham and the Jews are fulfilled through the Church, the New Israel, the New Covenant people of God. See Gen. 13:14 16; Gal. 3:6-9; 1 Pet. 2:9, 10.

Creation. (Gr. ktisis) Everything made by God. The term creation is applied to the cosmos in general and to mankind in particular. Our regeneration in Christ and the resurrection of the dead are both often called the "new creation." Creation has no existence apart from God, but is nevertheless distinct from God. (That which is not created, such as divine grace, the divine energies, belongs to God the Father, Son, and Holy Spirit.)

Creed. A statement of belief. Creeds in their earlier forms were used by the apostles, and many are recorded in the New Testament (Eph. 5:14; 1 Tim. 3:16; 2 Tim. 2:11-13). The creed used throughout the Church was adopted at the Council of Nicea in A.D. 325 and expanded at the Council of

Constantinople in A.D. 381. The Nicene Creed is used at baptisms, the Divine Liturgy, and in personal daily prayers.

Crosier. (Gr. *Ravdos* or *Pateritsa*). The pastoral staff of a bishop, signifying his responsibilities and the authority by which he spiritually rules his flock.

Crowns. (Gr. *Stephana*). A metal crown or wreath made of cloth in the shape of lemon blossoms, with which the priest "crowns" the newlyweds during the sacrament of Matrimony. The crowns are white, signifying purity, and represent the power that is given to the newlyweds to become "king and queen" of their home.

Crucifixion. A form of execution of criminals used by the ancient Romans in which the offender is nailed through his wrists and ankles to a cross. A crucified person usually died from suffocation after becoming too exhausted to pull himself up in order to breathe. Besides Christ Himself (Matt. 27:35-50), the Apostles Peter, Andrew, James the Less, and Simon were also crucified.

CRYPT - A crypt is an architectural feature found in churches of Europe, particularly in western Europe, that may be used as a chapel or a burial place. The crypt is located in the lower part of the church usually under the main floor, generally underground.

Cuffs. (Gr, EPIMANIKIA) Liturgical Vestments used by Deacons, Priests, and Bishops to wrap the sticharion sleeves and keeps them out of the way. They represent to the wearer that he does not celebrate the Liturgy, according to his own desires or strength, but must rely entirely on the strength of Almighty God.

CUPOLA - The steeple domes found on most Orthodox churches. There may be one cupola or as many as thirteen. One dome predominates and represents Christ as the head of the Church. On the roof of Orthodox churches are usually found one or more cupolas (towers with rounded or pointed roofs), called crests or summits.

CURTAIN - Drape over the Royal Doors of the Iconostasis.

Curse (Gr. anathema) To cut off, separate; the opposite of blessing. A divine curse is God's judgment. Christ delivers believers from the curse caused by their inability to live by the law of God (see Gen. 3:14-19; 9:25; Mark 11:21; Gal. 3:10-14). See Anathema.

CUSTOM - Established usage having the force of law. See also TRADITION.

-D-

Daily Cycle. The series of services served through out the day in an Orthodox Monastery or parish. The Evening Service (9th Hour, Vespers and Compline), The Morning Service (Nocturns, Matins and 1st Hour), and The Midday Service (3rd Hour, 6th Hour and Divine Liturgy or Typical Psalms). In addition, on Saturday evenings, as well as on Major Feasts, All-Night Vigil, which consists of a joining of Great Vespers and Matins into one Service, may be served. See Hours, Divine Liturgy, Compline Vespers & Vigil.

DAILY VESPERS - Daily Vespers is an abbreviated form of Great Vespers and is served on any day that Great Vespers is not appointed. Generally, Daily Vespers is served by a priest alone without the assistance of a deacon, although there is some variation in this practice

Damnation. Eternity spent in hell under sentence of personal condemnation for rejecting the love and truth of God as revealed perfectly in Jesus Christ and the Holy Spirit. See Matt. 25:31-46; John 3:18. see HELL

Darkness. A symbol of sin and rejection of God, who is light and whose followers walk in the light of righteousness. See John 1:5; Rom. 13:12.

Deacon. (Gr. "assistant, servant"). The first of the three orders of priesthood. Originally seven deacons were ordained to assist the apostles with the temporal affairs of the Church (Acts 6:1-7). This established office has continued in the Church. A deacon assists the bishop and priest, but cannot preside over the Eucharist, give blessings or pronounce absolution. In the New Testament (Rom.16:1) and the early Church, women also served as deacons or deaconesses but not in liturgical roles (1 Tim. 3:813). see deaconesses. Deacon are award title such as Protodeacon or Archdeacon. See ARCHDEACON.

Dean. (Gr. *Proistamenos*). An honorary title given to a presbyter, meaning:

> 1.the senior priest in a cathedral of a diocese;

> 2.the senior priest in a large parish or a deanery of parishes;

> 3.the head of the faculty in a theological seminary.

DEANERY - A territory consisting of several parishes, under the spiritual rule of a Dean. See DEAN.

DEATH - The death which came from the sin, of Adam is twofold: bodily, when the body loses the soul which quickened it, and spiritual, when the soul loses the grace of God, which quickened it with the higher and spiritual life.

The soul can die also, but not so as the body. The body, when it dies, loses sense, and is dissolved; the soul, when it dies by sin, loses spiritual light, joy, and happiness, but is not dissolved nor annihilated, but remains in a state of darkness, anguish, and suffering.

Deaconess. A pious lay woman assisting in the church as a caretaker or charity worker. The practice of using deaconesses in the Church was very ancient; however, it gradually disappeared.

DEFROCK. To deprive a priest or bishop of his Orders for a grave offense. See UNFROCK

Deification. The grace of God through which believers grow to become like Him and enjoy intimate communion with the Father through the Son in the Holy Spirit (see 2 Pet. 1; 2 Cor. 3:18; 5:17; 2 Pet. 1:2-4). This is the ultimate goal of salvation ask known as *Theosis*. See THEOSIS.

Departed. Those that have fallen asleep (the dead). Following death and judgment, those who have accepted God's truth and love as fully revealed in Christ and the Holy Spirit inherit eternal life in heaven. Those who have rejected His gift inherit eternal darkness. See Luke 16:19-31; Heb. 9:27.

Despondency. See AKEDIA

Deuterocanonical Books. The Old Testament that are accepted by the Orthodox Christian Church but are not accepted by Protestants as part of its official canonical contents, but of close association with the Bible. They are included in the Orthodox Bible because they were included in the Septuagint which was in use at the time of Jesus, and the authors of the New Testament. They are sometimes called apocrypha. See APOCRYPHA.

Devil. Satan, the leader of the fallen angels. Called by Jesus the father of lies John 8:44), Satan tempts the faithful to join his rebellion against God. The Greek word for devil means "separator"; he seeks to pull people away from God. Although not evil by nature, the devil turned by his free choice from what was according to nature to what was against it. At the end of time, Christ will judge the devil and his followers and cast them into hell. See Matt. 25:41; Luke 10:18; 1 Pet. 5:8.

Dikirotrikera. (Gr. "set of two and three candles" Dikiri and Trikiri). A set of two candleholders, one a double-branched candlestick and another a triple-branched, both used by the bishop in blessing at the liturgy. The *Dikeron* (double candleholder) signifies the two natures of Christ, while the *Trikeron* (triple candleholder) signifies the Holy Trinity.

DIASPORA - (Gr. exile) Faithful dispersed throughout the world.

Diocese. (Gr. *Episkopi*). The territory under the jurisdiction of a bishop. See SEE.

Diptychs. (Gr. "folding boards").

1.Lists of names of the living and dead, written down for their commemoration in the liturgy.

2.An official roster of the names of the heads of Orthodox jurisdictions read during the liturgy by concelebrating bishops or by the head of an ecclesiastical jurisdiction.

DISCIPLE - One of the Seventy followers (Luke 10:1) of our Lord, who were chosen in addition to the Twelve Apostles.

Discipleship. The life of learning, growing, self-sacrifice, and commitment required of every Christian. A Christian not only believes in Christ but leaves everything to follow Him. See Matt. 4:18-22; 7:21-23; Luke 9:23; Gal. 5:24.

Dismissal. (Gr. *Apolysis*; Sl. *Otpust*). The closing prayers and benediction, including the dismissal hymn (*Apolytikion*), in a church service. See BENEDICTION

DISPENSATION - The relaxing of a law in special circumstances. It can be granted by one in authority, a bishop or metropolitan for the redemption of individual believers. (see ECONOMY)

DIVORCE - While extending love and mercy to divorcees, the Orthodox Church is grieved by the tragedy and the pain divorce causes. Though marriage is understood as a sacrament, and thus accomplished by the grace of God and is permanent, the Church does not deal with divorce legalistically, but with compassion. After appropriate pastoral counsel, divorce may be allowed when avenues for reconciliation have been exhausted. If there is a remarriage, the service for a second marriage includes prayers of repentance over the earlier divorce, asking God's forgiveness and protection for the new union. A third marriage is generally not granted. Clergy who are divorced may be removed, at least for a time, from active ministry, and are not permitted to remarry if they are to remain in the ministry.

DOCETISM – The name of a heresy saying that Jesus was God, but only "appeared" to be human.

Doctrine. The teaching of the Church, called variously the doctrine of Christ (2 John 9), the apostles' doctrine (Acts 2:42), or sound doctrine (Titus 1:9; see 2 Tim. 3:16; Rom. 16:17).

Dogma. Basic beliefs and truths contained in the Bible and the Holy Tradition of the Church as defined by the Ecumenical Councils and the Fathers of the Church. Dogma is studied in the field of dogmatic theology.

Dogmatic. This is a musical composition sung at Vespers and are so named because they speak of the dogma of the Two Natures of Christ

DOMINION - A category of angelic beings. The dominions are so named because, being themselves free, they dominate over the rest of the angels that follow behind them. Having abandoned servile fear, as St. Dionysius the Areopagite says, they voluntarily and with joy serve God unceasingly. Also they send down power for prudent governing and wise management to authorities on the earth set up by God. Further they teach how to control the senses, how to subdue in oneself dissolute desires and passions, how to enslave the flesh to the spirit, and how to rule over one's will and be above all temptations.

DONATISM – The name of a heresy saying that the personal moral unworthiness invalidates the sacraments of clergy (even if repentant).

Dormition. in Slavonic "Ouspeniye." (see assumption).

DOVE - A common Christian symbol of the Holy Spirit, Who appeared in the form of a dove at the baptism of our Lord (MARK 1:10).

DOXOLOGY - A prayer of glory. The Great Doxology: Glory to God in the highest..." is sung at Matins; the Lessor Doxology: Glory to the Father . . ." is frequently used in our prayers.

-E-

Eagle. (Gr. *Dikephalos aitos*; Sl. *Orletz*). Small circular rug or permanent design on the church's floor, presenting a double-headed eagle with outstretched wings soaring over a city. It signifies the watchfulness and authority of the bishop over his diocese. The double-headed eagle was also the symbol of the Byzantine Empire.

EASTER. (Gr. *Pascha* or *Lambri*). The feast day of the resurrection of Christ, known also as "the Feast of Feasts" or simply Pascha (from the Hebrew word for Passover). Christ proclaimed Himself as the true Passover and offered Himself as a sacrifice. Orthodox Christians celebrate Pascha according to the decree of the Council of Nicea in A.D. 325: the first Sunday following the first full moon following the spring equinox following the Jewish Passover. Thus, Orthodox Pascha is often one, four, or five weeks after the western Pascha. See PASCHA.

Ecclesia. (Gr. "the gathering of the people").

　1.The gathering of the faithful at the church for worship and fellowship;

　2.The church where the liturgy is celebrated;

　3.The Church as the Body of Christ.

ECCLESIARCH - An ecclesiarch, or sacristan, in the Orthodox Christian Church is an officer of the church who is charged with the care of a church and its properties particularly in monasteries. His position resembles that of a sacrist in the Western Church. In large monasteries and

38

important churches the ecclesiarch may be assisted by a minor official called a paraecclesiarch.

Ecclesiastical. Whatever deals with or pertains to the Church and its life.

ECCLESIASTICAL YEAR - The ecclesiastical year, which according to Byzantine practice begins on the first of September, is divided between movable and immovable or fixed holy days. The movable holy days are determined by the date of Pascha - the most important of all feast days -, which is in a class by itself. The determination of the date of Pascha was definitively regulated by the decision of the First Ecumenical Synod, held in Nicaea (325). Next in importance to Pascha are the "twelve great feasts," of which three are movable. Eight of these feasts are devoted to Christ and four to the Virgin Mary. There are also a number of feast days of varying importance, most of which commemorate the more popular saints.

Ecclesiology. The branch of theology studying the nature, constitution, function, and membership of the Church.

ECONOMY - (oikonomia) 1) the management of a household. In theology the term refers first of all to God's providence as the divinity extends itself beyond the inner life of the Trinity: all that pertains to the created worlds and to the divine actions taken on their behalf and for their salvation. 2) Actions taken by the Church in the person of its officers (bishops, and by extension priests) for the redemption of individual believers in the sphere of Canon Law. While representing the Church's governing of souls and communication of grace, the canons are never in themselves absolute. They may be enforced literally, kat'akribeian, or with discretion, kat 'oikonomian, depending on the discernment of the needs of the particular soul. "Economy" of canonical application can therefore mean either a loosening of the canonical prescriptions (akin to the western term: "dispensation"), or the imposition of a discipline stricter than that which the canons provide.

Ecumenical Council. (see council).

Ecumenical Patriarchate. The Patriarch in Constantinople (Istanbul) who is know as the The "First Among Equals" of all the Orthodox autocephalous churches.

Ecumenism. is, principally, dialogue between Christian groups aimed at promoting the restoration of unity among all Christians through understanding, through mutual respect and toleration, and through practical cooperation in areas of common concern, such as care for the poor, sick, and needy. One has to welcome rejection of the age-old separation of Christians, but only if this is done with the objective of disclosing the treasures of Orthodoxy, to bring those who have fallen away from the Church back to unity in Orthodoxy. See BRANCH THEORY

ECUMENICAL MOVEMENT - (Ecumenism) An attempt by the Christian churches throughout the world to find some basis for the re-union of Christendom. See ECUMENISM

EIGHT TONES - A system of classifying liturgical poetry and melodies into eight categories, known as Tones. Derived originally from the Palestinian practice of singing Paschal hymns to a different melody (Tone) on each of the eight days of the feast, the Eight Tones came to be applied to eight week-long cycles of hymns. See Oktoechos.

Ektenia. (litany). A series of petitions chanted by the priest or deacon to each of which the choir responds. It is supplication or fervent prayer that comes out of the heart. These petitions call upon God's mercy. The response to an ektenial petition is "Lord have mercy."

EMINENCE, HIS - Title given to the Metropolitan and Archbishop.

EMMANUEL - (an appellation or Title of Jesus) "Therefore the Lord himself shall give you a sign; Behold, a virgin shall conceive, and bear a son, and shall call his name Immanuel. See Immanuel.

Encyclical. (Gr. "moving in a circle"; "circulating"). A letter by the head of an Orthodox jurisdiction (Archbishop or Patriarch) to those under his spiritual authority. The content of such a letter may vary, but it must refer to specific administrative or spiritual topics concerning the faithful.

Energy. Used theologically, that which radiates from the hidden essence or nature of God. The energies of God, such as grace, are not created, and allow the believer to enter into a personal relationship with God while preserving the unique character of God, whose essence always remains hidden from humanity. Moses was permitted to see the glory of God, His energies, but was forbidden to gaze on the face of God, His hidden essence. See Ex. 33:18-23; 2 Pet. 1:2-4. see GRACE.

Engainia. (Gr. "blessing for renewal"). The ceremony of consecration of a new church, conducted only by a bishop. It is performed before the Eucharist, and it mainly consists of the washing of the Holy Table of the altar, the depositing of relics in it, and the blessing of the church icons.

Engolpion. (Gr. "upon the chest"). The bishop's medallion, usually of enamel and richly decorated with precious stones, hanging upon his chest and signifying his episcopal office.

Entrance. (Gr. *Eisodos*). The solemn procession of the celebrating clergy carrying the Gospel at the liturgy, after the antiphons (Small Entrance), and carrying the Holy Gifts during the chanting of the cherubic hymn (Great Entrance).

Epanokalymafko. The monastic black veil hanging over the back of the *kalymafki* of a celibate Orthodox clergyman, especially the prelate of a church (see *kalymafki*). Some Orthodox prelates of Slavic background wear white *epanokalymafko*.

Eparchy. (Gr. "province, region"). An ecclesiastical jurisdiction headed by a bishop, metropolitan, or archbishop. see Diocese.

Epigonation. (Gr. "on the knee"; Sl. *Palitsa* or *Nabedrennik*). An oblong or rhomboidal vestment (approx. 12 x 12 inches) suspended from the belt and hung over the right side above the knee of a clergyman of higher rank. It signifies the cloth used by Christ to wipe his disciples' feet before the Last Supper and also signifies the sword of the Spirit, which is the Word of God.

Epiklesis. (Gr. *Epiklesis*). Special prayer or petition by the Priest to "invoke" or to call upon the Holy Spirit, in order that God's Grace will descend for the consecration of the Holy Gifts at the Eucharist.

EPIMANIKIA. See CUFFS

Epiphany. (Gr. *Theophania*; Sl. *Bogoyavleniye*). The feast in the Orthodox Church commemorating the baptism of Christ (January 6), and celebrating the "manifestation" of God in the Holy Trinity. See also THEOPHANY.

EPISCOPACY - The order of bishops in the Church (from Gr. episkopos, "overseer"). See also BISHOP.

EPISCOPATE - Collectively, the entire body of bishops.

Episkopos. The order of bishops in the Church (from Gr. episkopos, "overseer"). (see bishop).

Epitaphios. (Gr. "on the tomb"; Sl. *Plaschanitsa*).

1.The winding sheet on which the dead body of Christ is sewn or painted, representing his shroud.

2.An ornamented bier representing the tomb of Christ. On Good Friday, the Epitaphios is placed on the bier, which is adorned with flowers, and is carried in a procession representing the funeral of Christ.

3.The special service on Good Friday evening commemorating the burial of Christ.

EPISTLE - (Sl. Apostol) 1. Liturgical, A portion of the New Testament Scriptures read by the deacon or layman before the reading of the Gospel at Divine Liturgy. See APOSTLE.

Epitrachelion. (Gr. "about the neck"). One of the most important vestments, hanging from the neck down to the feet. An Orthodox priest must wear this particular vestment to perform a sacrament.

Equal to the Apostles. (Gr. *Isapostolos*). An honorary title given to saints such as St. Constantine and Sts. Cyril and Methodios for their missionary work in the Church.

Eschatology. (Gr. "the last things to happen"). The theological field concerned with life after death, especially the "last things," i.e., the state of the dead, the Second Coming of Christ, and the Final Judgment. According to the Holy Scriptures, Christ will come again at the end of time to judge the living and the dead, destroy the power of evil, and fully reveal the everlasting Kingdom (Matt. 25:3146; Rev. 20:10—21:1). See also SECOND COMING.

ESSENCE (Gr. ousia) Also translated as substance, nature or being. God the Father, the Son, and the Holy Spirit are "of one essence." Jesus Christ is "of one essence" with God the Father and the Holy Spirit in His divinity, and "of one essence" with all human beings in His humanity. God's essence is beyond the understanding and comprehension of His creatures. God can be known by humans through the divine energies and operations of the Father, Son, and Holy Spirit (Ex. 33:18-23). See also ENERGY.

ETERNAL LIFE 1) Life of the soul which continues without end after the death of the body. It is a life of blessedness for those who are saved, and suffering for those who are condemned.

ETHNOPHYLETISM — The name of a heresy saying that Church governance should be based on ethnic divisions, rather than geographic.

Eucharist. Taken from a Greek word meaning "thanksgiving," Eucharist designates Holy Communion, the central act of Christian worship. At the Last Supper Christ gave thanks (Matt. 26:27; 1 Cor. 11:24), and embodied in the communion service is our Own thanksgiving. The word came into use very early, as exemplified by its use in the writings of the apostles. (see Communion).

Euchologion. (Gr. "the book of prayers"; Sl. *Sluzhebnik*). A liturgical book used by the clergy, containing the various services, sacraments, and prayers required for the administration of sacraments and other ceremonies and services of the Church.

EVANGELIA (Sl.) - (Gr. Good News) The book containing the four Gospels from which the appointed lessons are read at Divine services. See GOSPELS

Evangelists. The authors of the Gospels (*Evangelia*), who, according to Church belief, were inspired by God in the writing of the Bible. The Evangelists are Matthew, Mark, Luke, and John. In the Orthodox Church, they are symbolically represented by a man, a lion, an ox, and an eagle, respectively.

EVLOGITARIA – These are Troparia sung at Matins and Funeral services, accompanied by: "Blessed art Thou, O Lord, teach me Thy statutes".

Exaposteilarion. (Gr. "dispatching"). A special hymn sung at Matins after the Canon. It refers to Christ's activity after the Resurrection, particularly His dispatching of the disciples to preach to the world.

Exapteryga. (Gr. "six-winged angels" Sl. *Ripida*). Metallic banners (fans) adorned with representations of angels, which are carried at various processions during church services.

Exarch. (Gr. "representative with full authority"). The head of an ecclesiastical jurisdiction, usually an Archbishop, representing the head of the Church (i.e., Patriarch) in the administration of a national Church.

EXCLAMATION - A prayer said aloud by a priest or bishop, which in most instances is the conclusion of a longer prayer said in a softer voice; one of the forms of ekphonesis.

Excommunication. (Gr. *Aphorismos*). Literally, "out of communion." This judgment is pronounced by the Church on willfully heretical, immoral, or divisive persons who refuse to repent of their sins, it excludes them from the sacramental life of the Church (1 Cor. 5:1-5) Excommunication is not viewed as eternal damnation but a discipline pertaining only to this life. It is administered for the salvation of the person cut off from communion, with the hope that this act will ultimately bring the sinner to repentance.. Church members may excommunicate themselves by absence from the sacraments and by actions contrary to Church law.

EXORCISM - Forbidding the devil to have any power over the newly baptized in the Sacrament of Baptism. The desire to be joined to Christ, confession of faith and worship of the Holy Trinity.

-F-

FAITH Belief and trust in Christ as one's Savior. The effects of this faith are freedom from the power of the devil, the attainment of virtue, and progress toward perfection and union with God. One is saved by faith through grace—a living faith manifested by a righteous life (see article, "Justification by Faith," at Rom. 5; Rom. 3:28; Gal. 2:16; Eph. 2:8; James 2:14 17).

FAITHFUL - Those who have been baptized and hold to the truths as members of the Orthodox Catholic Church.

FANS – see Exapteryga

FASTING An ascetic exercise whereby one gives up certain foods, usually meat and dairy products, as a means of disciplining the body. Fasting is a part of the ascetic life and a sign of repentance. Orthodox Christians fast on most Wednesdays and Fridays (in memory of the betrayal and crucifixion of Christ) and during four fasting seasons: (1) Advent, the forty days before Christmas; (2) Great Lent, forty days before Palm Sunday and the week before Pascha, (3) two weeks before the Feast of Ss. Peter and Paul (June 29); and (4) two weeks before the Feast of the Falling Asleep of the Virgin Mary (Aug. 15). See Matt. 6:16; Rom. 13:14; Gal. 5:16, 17.

FATHER (1) God the Father is one of the three Persons of the Holy Trinity. God the Son is eternally begotten of God the Father. God the Holy Spirit eternally proceeds from God the Father (see Matt. 28:19; John 14:10; 15:26). (2) "Father" is a title given to one's spiritual father or priest based on the custom of the Jews, who spoke of their father Abraham or their father David, and on the words of Paul, who called himself the father of his flock. See Luke 1:73; Acts 4:25 with center-column note; 1 Cor. 4:15.

FATHERS OF THE CHURCH - The teachers and defenders of the faith of the first six centuries who added notable holiness and complete Orthodoxy to their learning.

FEAST - A special day set apart for the liturgical commemoration of some saint, some event in the life of Christ, or in the life of the All Holy Virgin Mary. See MAJOR FEASTS

FELLOWSHIP (Gr. koinonia) Literally, "communion"; the unity of believers through Christ based on the fellowship of the Father, Son, and Holy Spirit. Christians are united into a special fellowship through their love for one another and common union with Christ (Acts 2:42; 1 John 1:3, 7). See also COMMUNION.

FILIOQUE A Latin word meaning "and the Son." Western churches began adding this word to the Nicene Creed several centuries after it was written: "I believe In the Holy Spirit . . . who proceeds from the Father and the Son." This "filioque clause" is judged by the Orthodox Church as error because it is contrary to what Jesus taught (John 15:26); thus, it confuses correct belief concerning the Holy Trinity. The addition of the filioque in the West was a major factor contributing to the Great Schism m A . D . 1054.

FILIOQUISM – The name of a heresy saying that the Holy Spirit proceeds from the Father and the Son.

FLESH (1) In New Testament usage, flesh refers to fallen human nature, which, through its ties to the world and mortality, struggles against spiritual growth and leads one into sin. Christians are called to subdue the lusts of the flesh so that they may grow in union with Christ (see Rom. 8:4 9; Gal. 5:16-24). (2) In Christology, flesh refers to the sinless human nature of Christ, or the Body of Christ. In liturgical usage, there is reference to the flesh of Christ in the Eucharist.

FOOL-FOR-CHRIST - One of the various customary saint titles used in commemoration at divine services when remembering saints on the Church Calendar. A saint known for his apparent, yet holy insanity.

FOREFEAST - A forefeast (also known as prefeast) is a period of time preceding certain major feasts of the Christian year during which the Church anticipates the approaching festival.

FORERUNNER - The glorious Prophet and Forerunner John the Baptist is also referred to as John the Forerunner because he was the forerunner of Christ.

FORGIVENESS: The remission of sin and guilt through the love of Christ. Forgiveness is given originally in baptism; forgiveness for continuing sin is reclaimed through repentance. As God has forgiven the sins of believers, so are Christians to forgive those who have sinned against them (Matt. 6:14, 15; 18:21-35; 1 John 1:9).

FORGIVENESS VESPERS - Forgiveness Vespers is served on the evening of Forgiveness Sunday and is the first service of Great Lent. Forgiveness Vespers follows the order of Lenten Sunday Vespers but after the Great Prokeimenon the clergy exchange their bright vestments for dark and the choir begins to use distinctive Lenten tones. Following the dismissal, the community celebrates the moving and beautiful rite of mutual forgiveness.

FORNICATION (Gr. porneia): The sin of sexual intercourse outside of marriage The word is also applied to polygamy and to many successive marriages. The Greek term means sexual immorality in general. Fornication is strongly condemned in Scripture (see 1 Cor. 6:16 18; Gal. 5:19; Col. 3:5.)

FREE WILL The freedom to choose between good and evil, between God and sin which is one aspect of humanity created in the image of God. According to Orthodox teaching, sin stains the image of God but does not destroy it. Human beings may choose to accept or reject the gospel, but must suffer the consequences of their decision (see Gen. 3:22, 23; Rev. 3:20).

FRUITS OF THE HOLY SPIRIT - Love, joy, peace, long-suffering, gentleness, goodness, faith, meekness, temperance (GAL. 5:22-23). see VIRTUES

FUNERAL SERVICE - A service for the burial of the departed, which essentially consists of the Memorial Service with the addition of a Gospel reading, special stichera on the Beatitudes and certain other stichera.

-G-

GENTILE A non-Jew. Christ and His Apostles preached the gospel first to the Jews, who were chosen by God to prepare the way for the Messiah. Christ died for all, Jew and Gentile; thus, salvation is offered to the Gentiles as well as to the Jews. Those Gentiles who believe in Christ become the true sons of Abraham, who was chosen by God before the Law was given. See Acts 11; 15:1-29; Rom. 1:16; Gal. 3:6-9.

GLORY - The divine splendor of God, or a specific manifestation of God's presence frequently likened to a cloud, smoke, or brilliant light. To serve and worship God is to glorify Him. Through the Holy Spirit, Christians are being changed to be like God and to reflect His glory. (Ex. 19:9, 16-18; Is. 60:1; Luke 2:9; Rom. 8:16 18; 2 Cor. 3:18; 4:6.)

GLOSSOLALIA Literally, "speaking in tongues." St. Paul uses the term to describe not an emotional experience but a spiritual gift (1 Cor. 12:10), though not one of the higher gifts (1 Cor. 14:1-5). At Pentecost the gift was given to allow those present to hear the gospel in their native language (Acts 2:6); in Corinth, the gift is an ecstatic utterance (1 Cor. 14:2). The Apostle warns against too much emphasis on this experience, urging instead that believers seek to manifest love (1 Cor. 13:1) and communicate the gospel intelligibly (1 Cor. 14:19). Glossolalia has never played a significant role in historic Orthodox spirituality. See 1 Cor. 12—14.

GNOSTICISM A very complex ancient heresy that was manifested in many different forms and beliefs. The Gnostics taught that Christ had imparted secret knowledge "gnosis," to a select few, who in turn transmitted hidden truths to an elite. Central to Gnosticism is the denial of the goodness of matter, leading to a denial of the reality of the Incarnation of the Son of God and of His bodily Resurrection. Several schools of Gnosticism taught that salvation consisted of liberation from the physical body and of growth to a higher, non-physical, spiritual level of existence. Orthodoxy has always rejected Gnosticism, teaching that the world and man were created good and will be redeemed by Christ and transformed at the end of this age (Gen. 1:1-31; Rom. 8:1922; I Cor. 15:35-55; Rev. 21:1).

GOD. The Supreme, Eternal and Almighty Spirit Who created all things and rules the universe. He is infinite in all perfections. He is One in Three Persons. The Orthodox Church teaches that we have knowledge of God, only because God has shown himself to his creation. God is the Lord and has revealed himself unto us; blessed is he who comes in the name of the Lord (Ps 117[118]:26-27). Also, God's self-revelation is found in His Son Jesus Christ, the fulfillment of the gradual and partial revelation of God in the Old Testament. Jesus is the one truly "blessed ... who comes in the name of the Lord." Orthodox Christians worship the Father, Son, and Holy Spirit—the Holy Trinity, the one God (Matt. 28:19; II Cor. 13:14; I Peter 1:1-2; Rom. 14:17-18, 15:16, etc.). see TRINITY

GOD THE FATHER is the fountainhead of the Holy Trinity. The Scriptures reveal the one God is Three Persons -- Father, Son, and Holy Spirit -- eternally sharing the one divine nature. From the Father the Son is begotten before all ages and all time *(Psalm 2:7; II Corinthians 11:31)*. It is from the Father that the Holy Spirit eternally proceeds *(John 15:26)*. God the Father created all things through the Son, in the Holy Spirit *(Genesis 1 and 2; John 1:3; Job 33:4),* and we are called to worship Him *(John 4:23)*. The Father loves us and sent His Son to give us everlasting life *(John 3:16)*. See TRINITY & FATHER

GOD-BEARER - One of the various customary saint titles used in commemoration at divine services when remembering saints on the Church Calendar. One who bears God within himself and is aflame in heart with love for Him.

God-parents. (Godfather, Gr. Nounos; Godmother, Gr. Nouna). Sponsors at Holy Baptism and Chrismation who undertake the responsibility for the faith of that person, thereby contracting spiritual relationship. For validity the sponsors must be Orthodox. The duties of the godparents are to take a permanent interest in the spiritual welfare of their godchildren and, if necessary, to undertake their religious education as far as they are able. The Orthodox people highly regard the spiritual bond and relationship between godparents and their godchildren, and marriage between them is prohibited (see affinity).

GOLDEN CANDLESTICK - (an appellation of the Theotokos) In the Old Testament Tabernacle, there were found in the Sanctuary golden candlesticks. The Theotokos is the Candlestick which held that Light that illumines the world (Ex. 25:31-40).

GOLDEN URN - (an appellation of the Theotokos) In the Old Testament, the Ark of the Covenant contained within itself a golden urn filled with the heavenly manna. The Theotokos is the Urn which contained Christ, the Divine Manna (Heb. 9:1-7).

GOLGOTHA - The Aramaic name for Mount Calvary where Christ was crucified.

GOSPEL Literally, "the good news." The term comes from the ancient title announcing the ascension of a new ruler to the throne. The Christian gospel is summarized in the statement, "Repent, for the kingdom of heaven is at hand!" (Matt. 3:2; 4:17). see BOOK OF GOSPELS

GOOD FRIDAY - (Sl. Great Friday) The Friday before Pascha Day on which the Church commemorates the death on the Cross of Jesus Christ. A very strict fast day. No Divine Liturgy on this day. (One exception, when the Feast of Annunciation falls on Good Friday, Divine Liturgy is celebrated.)

GRACE The gift of God's own presence and action in His creation. Through grace, God forgives sins and transforms the believer into His image and likeness. Grace is not merely unmerited favor—an attitude of God toward the believer. Grace is God's uncreated energy bestowed in the sacraments and is therefore truly experienced. A Christian is saved through grace, which is a gift of God and not a reward for good works. However, because grace changes a person, he or she will manifest the effects of grace through righteous living. See John 1:17; Rom. 5:21; Eph. 1:7; 2:8; 2 Thess. 1:12; 1 Pet. 5:5. see ENERGIES

GREAT ENTRANCE - the solemn procession during the singing of the Cherubic Hymn at Divine Liturgy, in which the bread and wine are transferred from the Table of Preparation to the Holy Table. (see Cherubic Hymn**)**

Great Feasts. Major celebrations throughout the liturgical year. While various saints and events are celebrated with significance on the local level, the entire Church celebrates together thirteen feasts above all the rest, Pascha (See Pascha) and the following **Twelve** Great Feasts.

Seven greats feasts in honor of our Lord Jesus Christ and five great feasts honoring the Theotokos constitute the Twelve Great Feasts.

- September 21 / September 8, the Nativity of the Theotokos
- September 27 / September 14, the Elevation of the Holy Cross
- December 4 / November 21, the Presentation of the Theotokos
- January 7 / December 25, the Nativity of Christ (Christmas)
- January 19 / January 6, Theophany, the Baptism of Christ
- February 15 / February 2, the Presentation of Christ
- April 7 / March 25, the Annunciation
- The Sunday before Pascha, Palm Sunday
- Forty Days after Pascha, the Ascension of Christ
- Fifty Days after Pascha, Pentecost
- August 19 / August 6, the Transfiguration
- August 28 / August 15, the Dormition (Falling Asleep) of the Theotokos

GREAT VESPERS - refers to the Vespers done the evening before a major feast day. Since Sunday is always the commemoration of the Day of Resurrection, Vespers on Saturday evening is always a Great Vespers. There are only minor variations between regular and Great Vespers, but generally there is more chanting as opposed to intoning various parts. See VESPERS

GREAT-MARTYR - One of the various customary saint titles used in commemoration at divine services when remembering saints on the Church Calendar. One who was martyred for the faith and suffered torture

Guardian Angel. (Gr. Phylakas Angelos). The Orthodox believe that certain angels are appointed by God at baptism to guide and protect each faithful person. A prayer of the Orthodox Liturgy asks for "an angel of Peace, a faithful guide and guardian of our soul and bodies."

-H-

HADES A Greek word equivalent to the Hebrew *Sheol* —"the realm of the dead". Following His burial and before His glorious Resurrection, Christ liberated the righteous dead in Hades, enabling them to enter Paradise because He had destroyed sin and death by His life-giving death (1 Pet. 3:18-20). Many English language bibles and text use the translation "Hell" interchangeably for this term. Though the term Hades is a more precise term according to the Greek.

Hagia Sophia. (Gr. Agia Sophia). The Church of the Holy Wisdom at Constantinople. Architecturally one of the greatest and most important churches in Christendom. Built under the Emperor Justinian in 532. After the capture of the city by the Turks in 1453 it was turned into a mosque, and since 1934 a museum.

Hagiography. (Gr. *Hagiologia*). The writings of the Church Fathers and the study of the lives of the saints. The Orthodox Church is a reservoir of such writings, which the faithful are urged to read for their spiritual growth and development.

HALO - (nimbus, type of mandorla) A circle of light pictured around the head of a saint to show holiness. The halo represents the light of divine grace suffusing the soul, which is perfectly united and in harmony with the physical body.

Hatjis. (or *Chatzis*; fem. *Hatjina*; Ar. "pilgrim"). A title or name given to those who made a pilgrimage to the Holy Land and are "baptized" in the Jordan River. Such a pilgrim may assume the title of Hatjis for the rest of his or her life. One also may attach this word before the baptismal name to produce a variation such as *Hatji-Yiorgis* or *Hatji-Yiannis*. Such names often become surnames, especially common among Greeks.

HEART In scriptural terms, the spiritual center of one's being. The heart is the seat of divine presence and grace and the source of moral acts. The transformation of the heart is the major work of God's saving grace. See Matt. 5:8; 6:21; 22:37; Luke 6:45; John 7:38; Rom. 2:29; 10:9, 10; Heb. 13:9.

HEAVEN is the place of God's throne, beyond time and space. It is the abode of God's angels, as well as of the saints who have passed from this life. We pray, "Our Father, who art in heaven..." Though Christians live in this world, they belong to the kingdom of heaven, and that kingdom is their true home. But heaven is not only for the future. Neither is it some distant place billions of light years away in a nebulous "great beyond". For the Orthodox, heaven is part of Christian life and worship. The very architecture of an Orthodox Church building is designed so that the building itself participates in the reality of heaven. The Eucharist is heavenly worship, heaven on earth. St. Paul teaches that we are raised up with Christ in heavenly places (Ephesians 2:6), "fellow citizens with the saints and members of the household of God" (Ephesians 2:19). At the end of the age, a new heaven and a new earth will be revealed (Revelation 21:1).

Hegoumenos. (see abbot).

HELL, (Hebrew, *Gehenna*) A place and state of condemnation in which the fallen angels and lost souls are tormented eternally for having willfully rejected the grace of God. See HADES & JUDGEMENT

Heresy. (Gr. "new and personal belief or idea"). Following one's own choice or opinion instead of divine truth preserved by the Church, so as to cause division among Christians. Heresy is a system of thought which contradicts true doctrine. It is false teaching, which all true Christians must reject (Matt. 7:15; 2 Pet. 2:1).

Hermit. (see *Anchorite*).

Hesychasm. A spiritual movement in the Byzantine Empire (fourteenth century) developed on Mount Athos, Greece. The term means "to be quiet" and signifies the system of spiritual development through meditation, contemplation, and perfection to the degree of absolute union with God (*theosis*). It is one of the forms of Orthodox Mysticism and is still practiced in the Orthodox world. see THEOSIS.

Heterodoxy. Different, alien, and presumably false belief or teaching. The Orthodox Church describes as such all other Christian denominations.

Hierarchy. The higher clergy or College of bishops who are assigned to rule over spiritual matters of the church.

HIEROMARTYR - One of the various customary saint titles used in commemoration at divine services when remembering saints on the Church Calendar. A martyr who is also a monastic clergyman.

HIGH PRIEST - (an appellation or Title of Jesus) "Seeing then that we have a great high priest, that is passed into the heavens, Jesus the Son of God, let us hold fast our profession." Heb 4:14

HOLY Literally, "set apart" or separated unto God; also, blessed, righteous, sinless. The word, therefore, refers to God as the source of holiness, to the Church and its sacraments, to worshipers of the true God, and to those of outstanding virtue. Those who are transformed by the Holy Spirit become holy as God is holy (Rom. 12:1; 1 Pet. 1:14 16; 2:9).

Holy Doors. See ROYAL DOORS

Holy Fire (Greek 'Αγιος Φως, literally "Holy Light") is a miracle that occurs every year at the Church of the Holy Sepulchre in Jerusalem on Holy Saturday, the day preceding Pascha. It is considered by many to be the longest-attested annual miracle in the Christian world, though the event has only been documented consecutively since 1106. see HOLY SEPLUCHRE

HOLY OBLATION - The Holy Oblation occurs on the Holy Altar, it is the part of the Divine Liturgy during which the Eucharistic elements are offered to God, and so become His Blood and Body.

HOLY OF HOLIES - (an appellation of the Theotokos) Into the Holy of Holies only the High Priest could enter. So too, the Theotokos is the Holy of Holies into which only the Eternal High Priest Christ entered (Heb. 9:1-7).

HOLY SCRIPTURE - Certain books written by the Spirit of God through men sanctified by God, called Prophets and Apostles. These books are commonly termed the Bible. In holy Scripture we read the words of the Prophets and Apostles precisely as if we were living with them and listening to them, although the latest of the sacred books were written a thousand and some hundred years before our time. See BIBLE.

Holy Sepulchre. The Church of the Resurrection (Anastasis), is a large Christian church within the Old City of Jerusalem. The ground the church rests on is venerated by many Christians as Golgotha, the Hill of Calvary where the New Testament records that Jesus Christ was crucified. It also contains the place where Jesus was buried (the sepulchre). The church has been an important pilgrimage destination since the 4th century, and the portions of it administered by the Orthodox are in the care of the Church of Jerusalem.

HOLY SPIRIT is one of the Persons of the Holy Trinity and is one in essence with the Father. Orthodox Christians repeatedly confess, "And I believe in the Holy Spirit, the Lord, the Giver of life, Who proceeds from the Father, Who together with the Father and the Son is worshipped and glorified..." He is called the "promise of the Father" *(Acts 1:4),* given by Christ as a gift to the Church, to empower the Church for service to God *(Acts 1:8),* to place God's love in our hearts *(Romans 5:5),* and to impart spiritual gifts *(I Corinthians 12:7-13)* and virtues *(Galatians 5:22, 23)* for Christian life and witness. Orthodox Christians believe the biblical promise that the Holy Spirit is given through chrismation (anointing) at baptism *(Acts 2:38).* We are to grow in our experience of the Holy Spirit for the rest of our lives. See TRINITY

HOLY TABLE -   This refers to the Holy Table (Altar Table) on which, at the Divine Liturgy, the Divine Food is offered. See ALTAR

HOLY TRADITION - the doctrine of the faith, the law of God, the sacraments, and the ritual as handed down by the true believers and worshipers of God by word and example from one to another, and from generation to generation. See TRADTION

Holy Water. (Gr. *Agiasmos*). Water blessed at the service of the "Great Blessing" on the feast day of Epiphany (Jan. 6) or on other occasions (Small Blessing). It is used for the blessing of people, as at Holy Communion, or for the blessing of things for their well-being.

HOLY UNCTION – see UNCTION

HOLY WEEK - (Passion Week) The week preceding Pascha in which the sufferings of Christ are commemorated. Each day of Holy Week has its own particular theme. See PASSION WEEK

HOMOSEXUALITY - The frequently used synonym, sodomy, comes from the apparent homosexual activity among men of Sodom (Genesis 19), and the severity of strictures set forth in the Holiness Code, with nothing short of the death penalty being imposed, suggested that the need for discipline must have been great, (Leviticus 18:22; 20:13). The Old Testament understood normal sexual intercourse as not only a way of expressing a loving relationship, but also as a divinely appointed way of procreating new life. In the New Testament, St. Paul condemns male prostitutes and homosexuals (I Corinthians 6:9-11). In the first chapter of his epistle to the Romans (Romans 1:24-32), he also judges it as unnatural. Patristic thinking, like scriptural references, were directed to the practice of homosexuality, not to the desire itself. The Orthodox Church does not condemn the person who keeps this propensity in check, and ministers to homosexuals who wish to find release from this inclination.

Holy Wisdom. (see *Hagia Sophia*).

HOPE An expectation of something desired. Christian hope is trust and confidence in the eternal goodness of God, a faith that Christ has overcome the suffering of this world. God is both the cause and goal of hope (John 16:20-24, 33; Rom. 5:2; 8:24, 25; 2 Thess. 2:16).

Horologion. (Gr. "Book of the Hours"; Sl. *Chasoslov*). The Liturgical book containing the services and prayers of the different hours of the day, i.e., Compline, Matins, Vespers, and the Office of the Hours (see hours).

Hours. In Orthodox monasteries & parishes, special services for the main hours of the day. Each hour commemorates a special event, as follows:

1.First hour (6:00 A.M.): Thanksgiving for the new morning and prayer for a sinless day.

2.Third hour (9:00 A.M.): the descent of the Holy Spirit on Pentecost.

3.Sixth hour (12:00 noon): the nailing of Christ to the Cross.

4.Ninth hour (3:00 P.M.): the death of Christ.

HYPOSTASIS A technical theological term for "person" or something which has an individual existence. The word is used to describe the three Persons of the Godhead: the Father, Son, and Holy Spirit. Hypostasis is also used to describe the one Person of Christ, who is both truly divine and truly human.

-I-

Icon. (Gr. "image"). Christ is "the image of the invisible God" (Col. 1:15). Because Christ is God who became Man, He can Himself be pictured or imaged. Thus, icons of Christ — together with those of His saints - express the reality of the Incarnation. Orthodox Christians honor or venerate icons, but never worship them, for worship is due to God alone. The honor given to icons passes on to the one represented on the icon, as a means of thanksgiving for what God has done in that person's life.

Iconoclasm. (Gr. "the breaking of icons"). It refers to the conflict in the Byzantine Empire between 727 and 843 over the use of icons in the church. The Seventh Ecumenical Council (787 and 843) decreed the use of icons, following in the main teaching of St. John of Damascus.

Iconography. The study and the art of painting of icons. In the Orthodox Church, iconography was developed mainly in the monasteries, which became the centers of its study and development.

Iconostasis. (Gr. "an icon-stand"). In the Orthodox Church, the term signifies:

1.The stand on which the main icon of the Patron Saint of the church is placed for veneration.

59

2.The screen separating the sanctuary or altar from the church proper and adorned with various icons. There may be two or three tiers of icons in an iconostasis, but the main tier must follow a certain iconographic form, as follows (from north, or left, side to south): the icon of the Patron Saint of the church, of the Virgin Mary, of Christ, and of St. John the Baptist.

ICXC - IC XC is an ancient Greek Christogram. This comes from the Greek spelling of Jesus Christ, IC XC is simply the first and last letter of each individual word. Often a bar is depicted over each to signify that it is an abbreviation and to signify Christ's divinity. In Orthodox iconography, IC XC will appear next to Christ's head. Notable also is that IC XC will appear next to Christ's head in Orthodox iconography.

IDOL A statue or other image of a false god; also, anything that is worshiped in place of the one true God. Money, possessions, fame, even family members can become idols if we put them ahead of God (see Lev. 26:1; Col. 3:5).

IDOLATRY - 1) Excessive or blind adoration, reverence, devotion, ect. 2) Religious worship of idols. See IDOL

Ikos. This is a short composition that follows the Kontakion, between the Sixth and Seventh Odes of the Canon.

Iliton. (or *Eiliton*, Gr.). The silk cloth used to wrap the corporal (or *antiminsion*).

ILLUMINATION Enlightenment. In the Bible, darkness is often used as an image of sin and death. To be illuminated is to be shown the true path of righteousness in God, thereby being led out of the darkness of sin and death. Baptism is called illumination, because in it we are delivered from sin and death and regenerated by the Holy Spirit. See Ezra 9:8; Ps. 13:3; 18:28; Eph. 1:18.

IMAGE (Gr. eikon) Literally, "icon." The Bible teaches that man was created in the image and likeness of God. Men and women reflect the divine image in their ability to reason and to rule nature, and in freedom of action. Although sin has darkened or stained God's image, it has not annihilated it. Through Christ, the image of God is renewed in man as believers are transformed by the grace of the Holy Spirit. See Gen. 1:26; Rom. 8:29; 2 Cor. 3:18. See also ICON.

IMMANUEL "God is with us," a title of Christ the Messiah, God in the flesh (Is. 7:14; Matt. 1:22, 23). see EMMANUEL

IMMERSION. In Baptism the submerging of the body in water. See BAPTISM

IMMORTALITY Eternal life. Those who follow Christ will rise to eternal life with Him in heaven; those who reject Him will be resurrected to eternity in hell (John 3:16-18; 5:26-29).

INCARNATE From Latin, meaning "to become flesh." Christ is God Incarnate: He became flesh—that is, human—thereby sanctifying human flesh and reuniting all humanity to God. According to Orthodox doctrine, Jesus Christ is perfect God and perfect Man (Luke 1:26 38; John 1:1-14; Phil. 2:5-7).

INCARNATION refers to Jesus Christ coming "in the flesh". The eternal Son of God the Father assumed to Himself a complete human nature from the Virgin Mary. He was (and is) one divine Person, fully possessing from God the Father the entirety of the divine nature, and in His coming in the flesh fully possessing a human nature from the Virgin Mary. By His Incarnation, the Son forever possesses two natures in His one Person. The Son of God, limitless in His divine nature, voluntarily and willingly accepted limitation in His humanity in which He experienced hunger, thirst, fatigue -- and ultimately, death. The Incarnation is indispensable to Christianity -- there is no Christianity without it. The Scriptures record, "...every spirit that does not confess that Jesus Christ has come in the flesh is not of God" *(I John 4:3)*. By His Incarnation, the Son of God redeemed human nature, a redemption made accessible to all who are joined to Him in His glorified humanity. SEE INCARNATE

INCENSE The sap of the frankincense tree, or other aromatic substances, dried and burned in honor of God. The offering of incense has been associated with the worship of God since God commanded Moses to burn incense to Him in the tabernacle. The prophet Malachi (1:11) predicts, "among the Gentiles [the Church] . . . incense shall be offered . . ." The Magi offered frankincense to the infant Christ. Incense manifests the prayers of the saints as they ascend to heaven. It is found in every revelation of the worship of God in heaven. See Ex. 30:1-8; Matt. 2:9-11; Rev. 5:8.

INFANT BAPTISM There are numerous biblical passages which support the ancient Christian practice of infant baptism, which was universal in the Church until the Anabaptist reaction after the Protestant Reformation. Among these are: "Let the little children come to Me, and do not forbid them; for of such is the kingdom of heaven" (Matt. 19:14); the baptism of whole households and families, presumably including children (Acts 16:14, 15, 25 33); and Paul's comparison between circumcision, which was given to infants, and baptism (Col. 2:11, 12). See John 3:3-6; Rom. 6:3, 4; Gal. 3:27; 1 Pet. 3:21.

INTERCESSION Supplication to God in behalf of another person. Christ intercedes before God the Father in behalf of the repentant sinner, and God's people intercede for one another (see Is. 53:12; Jer. 27:18; Rom. 8:34).

INTONE - To recite in a singing tone.

INVISIBLE - the word "invisible" in the Creed is meant the unseen, or Spiritual World, to which the Angels belong.

IRMOLOGION - This gives the text of the Irmoi sung at the beginning of the various Canticles of the Canon.

Irmos. This is the Theme Song of each Ode of the Canon. The word Irmos means link, since originally the Troparia that followed it were sung in the same rhythm, and thus were linked to it.

-J-

JESUS - The name "JESUS" means Savior. (See: JESUS CHRIST)

JESUS CHRIST is the Second Person of the Holy Trinity, eternally born of the Father. He became man, and thus He is at once fully God and fully man. His coming to earth was foretold in the Old Testament by the prophets. Because Jesus Christ is at the heart of Christianity, the Orthodox Church has given more attention to knowing Him than to anything or anyone else. See TRINITY

Jesus Prayer. A short prayer that the Orthodox constantly repeat to practice devotion to God; the tradition of repeating this distinctive prayer was developed in Orthodox monasteries. The text of the Jesus Prayer is: *"Lord Jesus Christ, Son of God, have mercy on me."*

JEW Originally one of God's chosen people who followed the covenant given to Moses by God. In the Old Testament, the Jews are (1) citizens of Judah; (2) the postexilic people of Israel; or (3) the worshipers of Yahweh. God chose the Jews to prepare the way for the coming of the Messiah, Jesus Christ, the Only Begotten Son of God. Through Christ the distinction between Jew and Gentile has been overcome, and all those who follow Him have become the true chosen people of God. See Acts 22:3; Rom. 1:16; 2:28, 29; Gal. 3:28; 1 Pet. 2:9.

JOY - Long term satisfaction, something positive to be anticipated in the future.

JUDAIZING – The name of a heresy saying Christians should become Jews first or more Jewish.

Judgment. In the biblical sense, God's decision on the worthiness of one to enter heaven or to be condemned to hell. Following death, all will be judged at the particular judgement. Christ will return again to confirm that this at the General or Universal Judgment. Because of sin, no one can earn a place in heaven by his own righteousness. However, through Christ, sin is forgiven and overcome, and those who have followed Him are granted a place in heaven. (Matt. 25:31 46; John 5:24; 16:8-11; Heb. 9:27; Rev. 20:11-15.)

JULIAN CALENDAR - The Julian Calendar was introduced in 46 BC by Julius Caesar and took force in 45 BC (709 ab urbe condita). It was developed in consultation with the Alexandrian astronomer Sosigenes and was probably designed to approximate the tropical year. It has a regular year of 365 days divided into 12 months, and a leap day is added to February every four years. Hence, the Julian Calendar's year is on average 365¼ days long. The Julian Calendar remains in use by the majority of Orthodox faithful for ecclesiastical dates. See CALENDAR.

Jurisdiction. (Gr. *Dikaiodosia*). 1) The right and the authority of a bishop to rule over his diocese as a spiritual overseer. It includes legislative, judicial, and executive authority, which can be exercised only by individuals who have been canonically ordained and appointed to rule over the jurisdiction in question. 2) A reference to self-governing churches.

JUSTIFICATION The act whereby God forgives the sins of a believer and begins to transform him or her into a righteous person. No person can earn justification by works of righteousness, for justification is the gift of God given to those who respond to the gospel with faith. God also helps those who cooperate with His grace to become righteous. Saving faith is not mere belief but a commitment to Christ that is manifested by works of righteousness (see Rom. 5; Rom. 5:1, 2; Gal. 2:16; Phil. 2:12, 13; James 2:24).

KAIRON - 'Time' or 'permission.' The prayers said by the clergy prior to the Liturgy in preparation for such service.

Kalymauki or kamilafki. (Sl. *kamilavka*). The cylindrical hat worn by Orthodox clergy. The black monastic veil (*epanokalynafkon*) worn by the celibate clergy at various services or ceremonies is attached to the *kalymauki* (see *Epanokalymafkon*).

Kanon.

> 1.Short hymns consisting of nine odes, sung at the service of Matins.

> 2.The special service known as the Great Kanon sung on the evening of the Wednesday of the fifth week of the Great Lent. See ODE

KATAVASIA (KATABASIA, 'Song of descension.') - in Greek this word implies the act of "descending" or "coming down." It is the name given to the hymn that concludes the ode of a Canon. During the singing of the Katavasia the two choirs are to "descend" from their places (the kliros) and assemble in the center of the church. The Katavasia may be the Irmos from another canon, or, as on Pascha, it may be the Irmos of the given ode repeated. These matters are regulated by the Typikon.

Kathisma. From the word kathizo I sit, these are selections from the Psalter, read at Vespers, Matins, and various other services, during which the Faithful are permitted to sit.

> 1.The twenty stanzas into which the Orthodox Psalter is divided.

Kathisma Hymn. These are short hymns sung after the Kathisma readings, during which the Faithful are permitted to sit (except for certain prescribed days). These are sometimes referred to as Sedalens or Sessional Hymns

KELLIA - Monk's room or cell in a monastery.

KENOSIS Literally, "emptying." The word is associated with humility or humiliation. God the Word humbled Himself by becoming man (with no change in His divinity), suffering death on the Cross for the world and its salvation (Phil. 2:5-8).

Kerygma. (Gr. "message; preaching"). Proclaiming or preaching the word of God in the manner of the Apostles. It is a method of church instruction centered mainly on Christ and the concept of salvation.

KINGDOM OF GOD God's rule over the world, showing (1) His absolute sovereignty as Creator and (2) His sovereignty over the faithful who voluntarily submit to Him. The Kingdom of God was made manifest by Christ and is present in the world through the Church. The fullness of the Kingdom will come when Christ returns to judge the living and the dead, creating a new heaven and earth. See Mark 1:15; John 3:3 5; Rom. 8:20, 21; 1 Cor. 6:9, 10; Rev. 21:1—22:5.

KISS OF PEACE A kiss on the cheek or the shoulder given by one believer to another as a sign of Christian unity and fellowship (see 1 Cor. 16:20). The clergy exchange the kiss of peace before saying the Nicene Creed during the Divine Liturgy of the Orthodox Church.

KLIROS - (also krilos) (pl. klirosi) (1) special areas, usually elevated, to the right and left sides of the iconostasis, where singers stand during the liturgy; (2) an ensemble of singers on the kliros.

KLOBUK - A klobuk is an item of non-liturgical clerical clothing worn by Orthodox Christian monastics and bishops who follow the Slav traditions. It is composed of a kamilavka covered with an epanokamelavkion (veil) that are attached to each other

KNOWLEDGE Knowing and experiencing the truth of God and salvation through Jesus Christ. Spiritual knowledge (1) is frequently identified with Christian doctrine; (2) is applied to the spiritual meaning of the

Scripture; and (3) refers to mystical and contemplative knowledge, not merely intellectual knowledge of God. Its aim and effects are to enhance man's responsibility, to aid in discernment of good and evil, and to lead people to God. See Luke 12:47, 48; 1 Cor. 13:2; 2 Cor. 4:6; Eph. 4: 16.

KOINONIA A Greek word meaning communion or intimate fellowship. This relationship exists between the three Persons of the Holy Trinity and also between Christians who are united by love into one body in Christ. See Acts 2:41, 42; 2 Cor. 13:14; 1 John 1:1-7. See also COMMUNION.

Kolymbethra. See BAPTIMAL FONT

Kontakion. A liturgical hymn that gives an abbreviated form of the meaning or history of the feast of a given day. The *kontakion* is sung after the sixth ode of the Canon in the liturgy and the Service of the Hours. St. Romanos the Melodist is considered to be the most important hymnographer of the *Kontakion*.

Koumbaros (fem. koumbara).

1.The "best man" in a wedding.

2.The sponsor in a baptism.(see God parent)

3.The address that Greek Orthodox use for their best man or their child's sponsor.

-L-

LADDER OF DIVINE ASCENT - The Ladder of Divine Ascent is an ascetical treatise on avoiding vice and practicing virtue so that at the end, salvation can be obtained. Written by Saint John Climacus initially for monastics, it has become one of the most highly influential and important works used by the Church as far as guiding the faithful to a God-centered life, second only to Holy Scripture.

Laity. (Gr. *Laikos*; Sl. *Miryane*). Members of the Church who are not ordained to the priesthood.

Lamb. (Gr. *Amnos*). The symbol for the sacrifice of Christ on the Cross (cf. John 1: 29). In the Orthodox liturgy, the amnos is the first square piece from the altar bread (prosphoro), inscribed with the letters ICXCNIKA (an abbreviated form for "Jesus Christ conquers"). This particular piece is to be consecrated during the Eucharist.

LAMB OF GOD Jesus Christ, the Lamb of God, offered Himself as a perfect sacrifice for the sins of the world (John 1:29). In the preparation service, the bread and wine are made ready to be consecrated in the Eucharist service to follow. The priest cuts out the center section of the loaf, called "the Lamb," for use in Communion as the Body of Christ.

Lamentations service. (Gr. *Epitaphios threnos*). Special hymns referring to the sacrifice of Christ on the cross and His burial (see *Epitaphios*).

Lampada. A lamp that is lit with oil, it is hanged in front of the icons, as a reference that Christ is the light Who illuminates the inside of His saints. See ICON

Lance or spear. (Gr. *Lonche*). A small, lance-shaped, double-edged knife used by the priest for the cutting of the altar bread in the service of the Preparation of the Holy Gifts (see *Proskomide*).

Language. According to the Orthodox tradition, the Church adopts and uses the language of any particular country or ethnic group that she serves. The main liturgical languages in the Orthodox Church are Greek, the various descendants of old Church Slavonic, and Arabic.

Last Supper. (Gr. *Mystikos Deipnos*; Sl. *Taynya Vercherya*). The last meal of Christ with His disciples in the

"Upper Room" before his arrest. With this supper, he instituted the Sacrament of the Holy Eucharist.

LAVRA - (laura) A type of monastery which is directly under the authority of the Patriarch, viz. Troitska Lavra in Moscow, Kievo-Pecherckaya Lavra in Kiev. A large, rich monastery of importance that has special privileges and is A cultural center in the region it occupies.

Leavened Bread. (Gr. *artos*). Bread made with yeast (*enzyma*) and used for altar bread for the Orthodox Eucharist (as opposed to the unleavened bread used by the Latin Church). In contrast to the Old Testament bread, which was unleavened to show the Israelites' separation from the world (see Ex. 12:15-20), leavened bread—risen bread—is used in Orthodox Communion to show forth the Resurrection of Christ.

LECTERN - A high movable reading desk of wood or metal with slanting top for reading the Gospel during Liturgy. It is brought in front of the Royal Doors on the Ambo and after the reading it is removed to the side. See ANALOGION

LECTIONARY - a book containing Scripture readings (pericopes) that are appointed to be read in Church services according to the cycles of the liturgical year. The lectionary goes back at least to the fourth century, and some of the oldest Greek manuscripts of the New Testament that have survived are Byzantine lectionaries. See PERICOPE

Lent. (Gr. *Sarakosti*). The fifty day fast preceding Pascha for the spiritual preparation of the faithful to observe the feast of the Resurrection. Besides Lent, the Orthodox Church has assigned a number of other fasting periods (see abstinence).

LIGHT The Bible frequently uses light as a symbol of God and of that which is good, that which overcomes the darkness of sin and death. Candles are used in churches to symbolize the light of Christ. Christians are lights shining in the world to show the way of righteousness and salvation (see Matt. 5:14; John 8:12).

Litany. A series of prayers, led by the Deacon, or in his absence, a Bishop or Preist, to which the people and the choir respond "Lord have mercy." See Ektenia.

LITIYA - (Lity, litia) A word implying a fervent, prolonged prayer. It is a service of blessing of the breads joined to the Vespers on the eve of major feasts. Five breads, oil and wine are blessed. In the prayer of blessing we ask our Lord that as He blessed the five loaves and fed the five thousand, to bless the loaves, wheat, wine and oil, and to multiply them in all the world; and to sanctify all the faithful who partake of them. The bread is cut and distributed to the faithful at the end of the service. See ARTOKLASIA

LITTLE ENTRANCE – (small or lesser) - A procession with the Gospel book during the first part of the Divine Liturgy, which begins during the third antiphon and concludes during the entrance hymn "Come, let us worship"

Liturgics. The theological field that studies the liturgies and the various services and rituals of the Church.

Liturgy. (Gr. "a public duty or work"). The main form of worship for the celebration of the Holy Eucharist. The Orthodox Church celebrates four different versions of the liturgy:

    1.The Liturgy of St. James,

    2.The Liturgy of St. Basil,

    3.The Liturgy of St. John Chrysostom, which is the most common, and

    4.The Liturgy of the Presanctified Gifts performed only during the period of Great Lent.

Logos. (Gr. "word"). A symbol for Christ, the word incarnate, or "word made Flesh," which is also called "the Word of God" (cf. John 1:1-4).

LORD - (an appellation or Title of Jesus) The Second Person of the Most Holy TRINITY is called "Lord" because He is as true God as God the Father.

Lord's Prayer. The prayer taught by Christ in the Sermon on the Mount (cf. Matt. 6: 9-33 and Luke 11: 2-4). It begins with the phrase "Our father..." and is the most common Orthodox prayer.

LOVE Charity, union, affection, friendship; unselfish concern for another's good. The love of Christians for each other and for the world is a reflection of the love between the three Persons of the Holy Trinity. See John 11:3, 36; 1 Cor. 13; 1 John 4:8, 16.

LXX (SEPTUAGINT) - The LXX was recognized as the authoritative Greek translation of the Jewish Scriptures and was read in the synagogues and churches of the Hellenistic world. Most Old Testament quotations in the New Testament are based on the LXX, not the Hebrew. Of particular interest is Paul's use of the LXX since, as a student of Gamaliel, he would have had ample knowledge of the difference between the Greek and Hebrew texts.

-M-

MAGI - (Sl. Volhvy) A name given to the "Wise Men from the East," who were guided by a star.

Magnificat. (Lat. "My soul doth magnify the Lord"; Gr. *Megalynalion*). A hymn of praise in honor of the Mother of God (*Theotokos*). Its verses follow Mary's own words beginning with the phrase "My soul doth magnify the Lord" (cf. Luke 1: 46-55). It is sung after the eighth Ode of the Canon at Matins.

MAJOR ORDERS - Major Orders in the Orthodox Church refers to the three degrees of ordained clergy: bishop, presbyter, and deacon. Persons who hold these offices are charged with the celebration of the divine services and the administration of Church life. They have received the grace of the Holy Spirit to perform these jobs through the mystery of Holy Orders. See ORDINATION

MAN (Gr. anthropos) Frequently used in the Bible in the generic sense for both man and woman. Man is the pinnacle of God's creation, for only he among the creatures was made in the image and likeness of God. See Gen. 1:26, 27; Luke 4:4.

MANICHAEISM – A heretical Persian Gnostic religion, highly dualistic.

MANTIA. See MANTLE

Mantle. (Gr. *Mandias Sl. Mantia*). A distinctive and elaborate garment, purple or blue in color, worn by the bishop in various church ceremonies and services, such as Vespers, but not during the liturgy.

MANDORLA - The mandorla or the nimbus is an iconographic symbol in the shape of a circle or an almond-shaped oval signifying heaven, Divine Glory, or Light. Mandorla is Italian for "almond." The mandorla is simply the iconographic way of representing heavenly glory, mystery, and majesty. see HALO

MARCIONISM – The name of a heresy that is the rejection of Hebrew "god" in favor of New Testament "god."

Marriage. Sacrament of the church joining man and woman together. It is not reduced to an exchange of vows or the establishment of a legal contract between the bride and groom. On the contrary, it is God joining a man and a woman into "one flesh" in a sense similar to the Church being joined to Christ (Ephesians 5:31, 32). The success of marriage cannot depend on mutual human promises, but on the promises and blessing of God. In the Orthodox marriage ceremony, the bride and groom offer their lives to Christ and to each other-literally as crowned martyrs

Martyr. (Gr. "witness"). Literally, "a witness." Normally, the term is used to describe those who give their lives for Christ. Martyria has two meanings: (1) witness or testimony, especially that which God bears to Christians, and which Christians bear to the world; and (2) martyrdom, especially Christ's Passion, and the martyrdom of Christians for the faith (see John 1:6-15; Acts 6:8—7:60).

Martyrika. (Gr. "a sign of witnessing"). Small decorative icons or crosses passed out to the guests who witness an Orthodox Baptism.

Martyrology. A catalogue of martyrs and other saints arranged according to the calendar.

MARY, THE ALL-HOLY VIRGIN is called *Theotokos,* meaning "God-bearer" or "the Mother of God", because she bore the Son of God in her womb and from her He took His humanity. Elizabeth, the mother of John the Baptist, recognized this reality when she called Mary, "the Mother of my Lord" *(Luke 1:43).* Mary said of herself, "All generations shall call me blessed" *(Luke 1:48).* So we, Orthodox, in our generation, call her blessed. Mary lived a chaste and holy life, and we honor her highly as the model of holiness, the first of the redeemed, the Mother of the new humanity in her Son. It is bewildering to Orthodox Christians that many professing Christians who claim to believe the Bible never call Mary blessed nor honor her who bore and raised God the Son in His human flesh. See THEOTOKOS

MASS - In the Western Church it is the service of the Eucharist. In the Orthodox Church this service is called the Divine Liturgy.

Matins. (Gr. *Orthros*). The Morning Service, which is combined with the liturgy. It begins with the reading of six psalms (*Exapsalmos*), the reading of the Gospel, the chanting of the Canon, and the Great Doxology.

MATUSHKA (Sl.) - (Gr. Presbytera) The wife of a Priest is addressed in this manner. The word is an endearing term for "mother." see Presvytera

MEDIATOR One who intervenes on behalf of another. Jesus Christ intervenes on behalf of the faithful before God the Father (1 Tim. 2:5).

Memorial. (Gr. *Mnymosyno*). A special service held in the Orthodox Church for the repose of the souls of the dead. Memorial services are held on the third, ninth, and fortieth day; after six months; and one or three years after death. Boiled wheat is used as a symbol of the resurrection of everyone at the Second Coming of Christ.

MEMORY ETERNAL - (Sl. Vichnaya Pamyat) This hymn is taken from the Gospel accounts of Jesus' crucifixion. The Lord is crucified with two thieves one mocks Him with the crowd gathered to see Jesus on the cross, but the other repents of his sins and says to Jesus, "Remember me when You come in Your Kingdom." (Luke 23:42) Jesus replies, "Very truly I tell you, today you shall be with me in Paradise." (Luke 23:43) As we sing "Memory eternal" for our departed loved-ones, we are saying, "Remember them, Lord, when You come in Your Kingdom".

Menaion. A liturgical book containing the lives of the saints and the special hymns (*stichera*) for the feast-days of the Orthodox Saints. It is divided into twelve volumes, one for each month. In addition, there is sometimes found two companion volumes which contain certain texts from the major Fixed Feasts (the Festal Menaion) or general Offices for certain classes of Saints (the General Menaion).

MERCY The compassionate, steadfast love of God for sinners. Christians reflect the mercy of God by caring for others. The most frequent prayer in Orthodox worship is "Lord, have mercy." See Matt. 5:7; Eph. 2:v7; Titus 3:4 7.

MESSIAH The Christ, the anointed one of God. Jesus Christ is the Messiah, fulfilling all the promises made by God to His chosen people (see Is. 7:14; 9:6; Matt. 16:13 17). see JESUS CHRIST

METANOIA — 1) A little prostration made by bending down to touch the ground with your hand. 2) Also means to change ones mind; to repent. See REPENTANCE

Metropolitan. The head archbishop of an ecclesiastical province, with primacy of jurisdiction. As a mark of distinction the Metropolitan wears a white klobuk with a cross on it. The title of archbishop or metropolitan may be granted to a senior bishop, usually one who is in charge of a large ecclesiastical jurisdiction. He may or may not have provincial oversight of suffragan bishops. He may or may not have auxiliary bishops assisting him. In the Slavonic and Antiochian traditions, a metropolitan outranks an archbishop. The reverse is the situation in the Greek tradition.

MIDNIGHT OFFICE - (Greek, Mesonyktikon; Slavonic, Polúnoschnitsa) is part of the Daily Cycle of services in the Orthodox Church. The office originated as a purely monastic devotion inspired by Psalm 118:62 (119:62 KJV), "At midnight I arose to give thanks unto Thee for the judgments of Thy righteousness," and also by the Gospel parable of the Wise and Foolish Virgins (Matthew 25:1-13). The name of the Midnight Office is sometimes translated as "Nocturns," a term borrowed from the Western liturgical tradition; but it should be noted that in the West "Nocturn" refers to a division within the completely different office of Matins.

MILITARY CHAPLAINS - Priests who have been granted permission to serve the spiritual needs of military personnel.

MILLENNIUM - A thousand years. The Orthodox Church has traditionally taught that the thousand-year reign of Christ on earth before the final defeat of Satan, as recorded in Rev. 20:1-3, is symbolic of the rule of Christ through the Church, which is a manifestation of the Kingdom of God (2 Pet. 3:8). see CHILLIASM

MIND The intelligent faculty, the inner person; often used synonymously with "heart." There are two Greek words for mind: (1) nous, the mind which is separated from the sensible world and the passions (Rom. 8:7; 12:2); and (2) dianoia, the intellect (Matt. 22:37). see NOUS

MIRACLE A sign whereby God supersedes the normal laws of nature in a mysterious way in order to manifest His power as Master of the universe. Jesus Christ performed many miracles—some showing His mastery over nature, others demonstrating His power over sin, disease, and death. The apostles continued to manifest the power of God through miracles. Healings, weeping icons, and other contemporary miracles also show His power in the world today. See Matt. 8:1-34; John 11:144; Acts 3:1-9.

MISSION A task given by God to His people. Christ sent the Seventy on a mission (Luke 10:1-24). St. Paul went on three missionary journeys to preach the gospel (Acts 13:1—14:28; 15:36—18:22; 18:23 21:16). The mission of the Church today is to proclaim Christ to the world.

MISSIONARY - One who is sent, whether Bishop, Priest or Layman, to do the work of the Church where it has not been established.

Mitre. (Gr. *Mitra*). The official headdress or "crown" of a bishop. In Slavic churches, some Archimandrites an Archpriests are allowed to wear the mitre as a recognition of their service to the church (*mitrate* or *mitrophoros*). The mitre derives from the crown of the Byzantine emperor.

MIXED MARRIAGE - A marriage between an Orthodox and a non-Orthodox.

MOLEBEN - Molieben (from Church Slavonic Mol'ba - prayer, supplication) *(L. Te Deum) (Gr. Paraklesis)* A service of thanksgiving for favors received, or prayers of petition for protection from misfortune. It is a short liturgical service usually centered on a particular need or occasion: the new year, a journey, an illness, an act of thanksgiving, etc. It may be addressed to Christ, the Mother of God, or to saints. Its general structure is that of Matins, and it can be served either by request of the faithful or by decision of the parish Priest.

Monastery. The dwelling place and the community thereof of monks or nuns living together in a communal life (*cenobites*) in a convent and practicing the rules of prayer and vows. The members of some monasteries live alone in solitude (*anchorites*).

Monasticism. The state on being a Monk in various systems: 1- Solitude (Hermits): a monk lives in a cell or cave. 2- Coenobitic discipline where monks live together, participating in some prayers and eat together. 3- Communal Order: where groups of monks live together having the same spiritual father. They live in separate cells apart from each other. They meet together weekly, on Saturdays and Sundays. See ANCHORITES, MONASTERY, MONK.

Monk. (Gr. *Monachos*; fem. *Monache*). An individual who denies the world in order to live a religious life under the monastic vows of poverty, chastity, and obedience.

MONOENERGISM – The name of a heresy saying that Jesus had only one energy, the divine.

Monophysitism. A heresy which arose in the fifth century concerning the two Natures of Christ. The monophysites accepted only the Divine Nature of Christ and were condemned as heretics by the Fourth Ecumenical Council, at Nicaea (451 A.D.) (see also Copts).

MONOTHEISM - the doctrine or belief that there is only one God.

Monothelitism. A heresy of the seventh century, which developed in an attempt to reconcile the monophysites with the Orthodox. The monothelites accept the two Natures of Christ, but deny His human will (*Thelesis*), accepting thereby only his Divine.

Mortal Sins. (see capital sins).

MOTHER OF GOD (Gr. Theotokos) The Virgin Mary gave birth to Jesus Christ, the Son of God. She is therefore the Mother of God. This is the teaching of the Orthodox Church denned by the Council of Ephesus in 431. It does not mean that Mary generated the Godhead, for the Word (the Son of God) was in the beginning (JOHN 1:1). It means that the Virgin Mary was the Mother of the Person who is God. This is her fundamental dignity, and the origin and justification of all the honor which is bestowed on her by the Orthodox Church. See THEOTOKOS

MOTHER CHURCH - 1) The Church of Jerusalem, as being the first Christian Church. 2) The church that granted autocephalous or autonomous status to create another church from one of its own diocese.

Mount Athos. The center of Orthodox monasticism, situated on a conical mountain on the Chakidi Peninsula, Greece.

MYRRH - (Chrysm) The sacred oil which is used for annointing in the Sacrament of Chrysmation. This sacred oil is a mixture of many substances and is made by several bishops on Holy Thursday. See CHRISM

MYRRH-BEARER - (1)One of the various customary saint titles used in commemoration at divine services when remembering saints on the Church Calendar. (2) One of the women who were present at Christ's passion and went to the tomb to anoint the body of Jesus.

MYRRH-STREAMING - One of the various customary saint titles used in commemoration at divine services when remembering saints on the Church Calendar. Myrrh-streaming, Myrrh-gusher, or Myroblete: the relics of the saint exude holy and sweet-smelling (and often miraculous) oil.

MYSTERY The ways of God, especially God's plan for salvation, which cannot be known with the rational, finite human mind, but can be experienced only by the revelation of God. The Orthodox Church also uses the term mystery for the sacraments of the Church. See Mark 4:11; 1 Cor. 2:7, 8; Eph. 5:32. see also SACRAMENT.

Mysticism. The search through various prayers and practices to achieve unity with God in life (*theosis*) (see hesychasm).

NABEDRENNIK - (Epigonation) A part of the priestly vestment in the Slavic usage which is suspended upon the left hip signifying the Sword of the Spirit, which is the Word of God.

Name-day. (Gr. *Onomastiria* or *Onomastiki eorti*). The tradition of the Orthodox people is to celebrate one's name-day instead of a birthday. Since the Orthodox people are usually named after a saint's name, all those having the same name celebrate together. Celebration of the name-day is considered to be spiritually important, and the celebrating individual develops special spiritual ties with his Patron Saint and consequently, with God.

Nativity. The name is used to designate three feasts: the birth of our Lord (Dec. 25), the birth of the All Holy Virgin (Sept. 8), and the birth of St. John the Baptist (June 24). These are the only actual birthdays kept by the Church. See INCARNATION.

NATIVITY FAST - (Advent) The Nativity Fast is one of the four Canonical Fasting Seasons in the Church year. This is a joyous fast in anticipation of the Nativity of Christ. That is the reason it is less strict than other fasting periods. The six weeks prior to Christmas (the Nativity of our Lord in the Flesh) is a fasting period that many call Advent. Advent means "coming." The fast is also called St. Philip's Fast, coming immediately after his feast on November 14. see ADVENT & ABSTINENCE

Narthex. The vestibule area of the church, leading to the church proper or the nave. In the early Church, this area was assigned for penitents and those who were not yet baptized (catechumens).

NATURE The sum of the qualities shared by individuals of the same type. (The qualities which distinguish individuals of a type from one another make up the "person.") The Holy Trinity is one divine Nature in three Persons. Humanity is one human nature in many persons. Although stained by sin, human nature is good, having been created in the image of God. Through grace, the Holy Spirit restores the nature of believers to its true, uncorrupted state, so that they may grow into union with God. See Gen. 1:2631; 2 Cor. 3:18; 5:17.

Nave. The center, the church proper of an Orthodox Church, where the faithful remain to observe the liturgy and other services.

Neophyte. (Gr. *Neophotistos*). A newly baptized individual or convert of the early Church.

NESTORIANISM - The name of a Christological heresy which originated in the Church in the 5th century out of an attempt to rationally explain and understand the incarnation of the divine Logos, the Second Person of the Holy Trinity as the man Jesus Christ. Nestorianism teaches that the human and divine essences of Christ are separate and that there are two persons, the man Jesus Christ and the divine Logos, which dwelt in the man. Thus, Nestorians reject such terminology as "God suffered" or "God was crucified", because they believe that the man Jesus Christ suffered. Likewise, they reject the term Theotokos (Giver of birth to God) for the Virgin Mary, using instead the term Christotokos (giver of birth to Christ) or Anthropotokos (giver of birth to a man).

New Calendar. The Gregorian calendar is the calendar in contemporary use in most countries. During the Middle Ages, some problems were discovered with the use of the Julian Calendar: every century had three to four days too many. In the sixteenth century the mistake grew to 10 days. Therefore, in 1582, it was decided that the calendar needed reform. Pope Gregory XIII decreed that October 4 should be followed by October 15 at once. Also, he decided that all of the leap days of the full century years which were not dividable by 400 would be omitted. In this manner, 1900 was not a leap year, 2000 was a leap year, and 2100 will not be. The average duration of the Gregorian year is 365.2425 days. See CALENDAR & GREGORIAN CALENDAR

NEW MAN One who is being transformed or deified by the Holy Spirit into a new creature in communion with God (2 Cor. 5:17; Gal. 6:15).

NEW JERUSALEM The center of the Kingdom of God which will be established following the Second Coming of Christ and the Last Judgment. The heavenly Jerusalem will take the place of the old earthly Jerusalem, and is called by Paul, "the mother of us all" (Gal. 4:26). See Rev. 3:12; 21:2.

NEW MARTYR - One of the various customary saint titles used in commemoration at divine services when remembering saints on the Church Calendar. The title of New Martyr was originally given to martyrs under heretical rulers (the original martyrs being under pagans), then later to the Church's martyrs under Islam and various modern atheistic regimes, especially Communist.

NEW TESTAMENT - The books of the Bible which contain the revelation of God since the coming of Christ: the four Gospels, the Acts of the Apostles, the seven General Epistles, the fourteen Epistles of Saint Paul, and the Book of Revelation (Apocalypse). See BIBLE

NICENE CREED - The statement of the Orthodox Christian faith expressed in twelve articles. This formula of the confession of faith was made at the first Council of Nicea (in 325) and expanded at the first Council of Constantinople (in 381). The Western Church made an alteration in this original form by adding the Filioque, which is one of the stumbling blocks between the Roman Church and the Orthodox Church. See CREED

NIMBUS - A nimbus can also refer to the halos of light around the heads of angels and saints in icons. Also in icons, Christ's nimbus (halo) carries the cross and contains the Greek words meaning He Who Is. See HALO.

NOCTURNE - Nocturne is the midnight service of the Church. See MIDNIGHT OFFICE

NON-CHALCEDONIANISM - Non-Chalcedonianism is the view(s) of those churches that do not accept the

Confession of Chalcedon as defined at the Ecumenical Council of Chalcedon of 451. Some Christian denominations accept the doctrines of the previous council at Ephesus in 431, but do not accept, for varying reasons, the teachings of Chalcedon. The most substantial Non-Chalcedonian tradition is known as Oriental Orthodoxy. Within this tradition are a number of ancient Christian churches including the Coptic Orthodox, the Syriac Orthodox (sometimes referred to as "Jacobite"), the Armenian Apostolic, the Ethiopian Orthodox, the Eritrean Orthodox and the Malankara (Indian) Orthodox.

Nounos. (see god-parents).

NOUS - The nous is our highest faculty. It has been called: the "eye of the psyche," the "eye of the heart," and also the "energy of the psyche." When cleansed, the nous resides and operates from within the heart; it can perceive God and the spiritual principals that underlie creation; it is cognitive, visionary, and intuitive.

NOVATIANISM – The name of a heresy saying that people who apostasize or commit serious sin can never be absolved.

Novice. (Gr. *Dokimos*). An individual who accepted the monastic life, undergoing a period of probation in preparation for taking his vows.

Nun. (Gr. *Monachi* (fem), or *Kalogria*). A woman following the monastic life, living in a convent and leading a strict contemplative

NUNC DIMITIS - Two Latin words beginning the Song of Simeon (Luke 2:29-32) sung at Vespers : "Now lettest Thou Thy servant depart"

Oblation. Proskomedia. A service of preparation of the elements of bread and wine before the beginning of Divine Liturgy, (b) Table of Oblation (Sl. Zhertvennik) The table on the left side of the Sanctuary where the preparation of the elements is made. (see *Proskomide*).

OCTAVE - The commemoration of a feast over a period of eight days from the day of the feast to the Apodosis (Otdaniye). See APODOSIS & AFTERFEAST

ODE - (Sl. Irmos) Biblical Odes (also called canticles) One of the nine canticles of the canon sung at Matins. They are nine hymns that are taken directly from Scripture. Originally, these odes were chanted in their entirety every day, with a short refrain inserted between each verse. Eventually, short verses (troparia) were composed to replace these refrains, a process traditionally inaugurated by Saint Andrew of Crete.? Gradually over the centuries, the verses of the Biblical Canticles were omitted (except for the Magnificat), and only the composed troparia were read, linked to the original canticles by an irmos. During Great Lent, however, the original Biblical Canticles are still read. see IRMOS & KANON

Offertory. (see *Proskomide*).

Oikonomia. See ECONOMY

Oktoechos. (Gr. "eight modes" or *Paraklitiki*). Service book containing the canons and hymns of the eight tones or modes of Byzantine music. They are used in all services, arranged every eight weeks, one for each tone, and are attributed to St. John of Damascus (eighth century), one of the greatest Orthodox hymnographers and theologians.

OLD BELIEVERS - In the context of Russian Orthodox church history, the Old Believers became separated after 1666-1667 from the hierarchy of the Church of Russia as a protest against church reforms introduced by Patriarch Nikon of Moscow. Old Believers continue liturgical practices which the Russian Orthodox Church maintained before the implementation of these reforms. Because of the use of these older liturgical practices, they are also known as Old Ritualists. - Russian-speakers refer to the schism itself as raskol (etymologically indicating a "cleaving-apart"). See OLD RITE.

OLD MAN One not transformed by the Holy Spirit, still a slave to sin and death (Rom. 6:5 7; Eph. 4:20 24).

Old Rite . Russian Orthodox Christians who have preserved the Old Rite following the liturgical reforms of Patriarch Nikon in the second half of seventeenth century (Old Believers).

Omophor. (see Pall).

Orarion. (Lat.) One of the deacon's vestments, made of a long band of brocade and worn over the left shoulder and under the right arm. It signifies the wings of the angels.

Ordination. (Gr. *cheirotonia*). The sacrament of the Holy Orders, imparted through the laying on of hands upon the candidate for bishops, priests, and deacons; exist to make manifest in the Church the divine life of the Kingdom of God to all men while still living in this world.

Oriental Orthodox. See Monophysitism

Orientation - Towards the East, Since the early days of Christianity, the east has been the direction designated to be faced during prayers, both by the officiating priest and by the congregation. This has to be taken into account in building a church, so the altar must be placed in the eastern end, with the longer axis of the church running east to west.

ORIGINAL SIN The fact that every person born comes into the world stained with the consequences of the sins of Adam and Eve and of their other ancestors (Ancestral Sin). These consequences are chiefly: (1) mortality, (2) a tendency to sin, and (3) alienation from God and from other people. Original sin does not carry guilt, however, for a person is guilty only of his or her own sins, not of those of Adam. Therefore, the Orthodox Church does not believe that a baby who dies unbaptized is condemned to hell. (Gen. 3:1-24; Rom. 5:12-16.)

Orthodox. (Gr. "correct or true belief"). The common and official name used by the Greek Christians and Paschan Christian Church. The Orthodox Church maintains Her belief that She alone has kept the true Christian faith, complete and unaltered.

ORTHODOX CHRISTIAN CHURCH - The Church established by our Lord Jesus Christ, propagated by His Apostles and handed down by the true believers by word and example from one generation to another. The Church includes several Patriarchates. Originally there were five Patriarchates ; Constantinople, Alexandria, Antioch, Jerusalem and Rome. In 1054 the Roman Patriarchate separated from the Orthodox Church. The Orthodox Church is One, Holy, Catholic and Apostolic.

Orthodox Sunday. The first Sunday of Lent, commemorating the restoration of icons in the church (see Iconoclasm).

Orthros. (Gr. daybreak) The morning service usually called Matins. It consists principally of six psalms (3, 37, 62, 87, 102, 142), a litany, troparion, kathisma, a Gospel and the Canon. (see Matins).

PAGAN - For the early Christians, a pagan was a believer in polytheistic religion.

Paganism. Belief in religions other than Christianity, especially ancient Greek polytheism, which was a non-revealed religion.

PALITSA - (Epigonation) Part of the sacred vestments - a diamond-shaped piece worn by the Archpriest or bishop on the right side. It is given to the Archpriest as an award for devoted service to his priestly duties. In the Greek church this is given as a distinction to those priests that are blessed to hear confessions. See Epigonation

Pall. (Gr. *Omophorion*). One of the bishop's vestments, made of a band of brocade, worn about the neck and around the shoulders. It signifies the Good Shepherd and the spiritual authority of a bishop.

Palm Sunday. (Gr. *Kyriaki ton Vaion*; Sl. *Verbnoye Voskresenye*). The Sunday before Pascha, commemorating the triumphal entrance of Christ into Jerusalem. The Orthodox use palms or willow branches in the shape of a cross, which the priest distributes to the faithful after the liturgy.

Panagia. (Gr. "All Holy"). One of the Orthodox names used to address the Mother of God. In Orthodox art, the term Panagia denotes an icon depicting the Virgin Mary with the Christ Child, or the bishop's medallion (*Encolpion*) which usually is decorated with an icon of the Panagia (especially in the Russian Church). (See also *Theotokos*.)

Pannikhida. (Pannykhida) A service for the repose of the souls of the departed faithful. See MEMORIAL

Pantocrator. (Gr. "He who reigns over all; almighty"). One of the appellations of God. In Orthodox art, Pantocrator is the name of the fresco decorating the center of the dome, depicting Christ as the almighty God and Lord of the Universe.

PARABLE A story told to illustrate a greater truth through images related to the daily lives of the hearers. Christ's teaching is filled with parables.

PARADISE The place of rest for the departed in Christ. The original Paradise, seen in Gen. 2:8 14, will be restored in its fullness following the Second Coming of Christ. See Luke 23:43; 2 Cor. 12:4; 2 Pet. 3:13; Rev. 2:7; 21:1.

PARADOX That which is true, but not conventionally logical: for example, that a virgin could bear a Son and yet remain a virgin, as did Mary; or that God can be One, yet three Persons. The Christian faith is full of paradoxes, because our intellect is not sufficient to comprehend the mind of God (see Is. 55:8, 9).

PARAKLESIS - A paraklesis is a service of supplication specifically for the living as opposed to a Memorial Service, which is a supplication for the departed. This service is most often addressed to the Theotokos, but may be used to seek the intercessions of any saint. The distinguishing feature of a paraklesis is the inclusion of a supplicatory canon to the saint whose intercessions are being sought. A paraklesis can be served as a stand-alone service or, in a slightly abbreviated form, in conjunction with Vespers. It is appropriate to be served at any time of need. In Slavic practice, there is a similar service that is called a "moleben" this service is either served as a stand-alone service or in conjunction with the Divine Liturgy. See MOLEBEN.

PARASTAS - A solemn service for the repose of departed as a memorial to them, longer and more complete than the Pannikhida.

Paraklitiki. (see *Oktoechos*).

PARISH - Group of faithful united under a properly ordained priest to form a unit of a Diocese, acceding to the Canons, Traditions, Doctrines, discipline and Divine Sacraments of the Orthodox Church.

PARTICLES - Small pieces taken out of the prosphora and placed on the paten at the Proskomedia. The particles are in honer of Most Holy Virgin Mary, nine ranks of saints, and those commemorating the faithful living and dead. See PROSKOMIDE

Pascha. Greek for "Passover." Originally Pascha designated the Jewish Passover; now, it is the Feast of the Resurrection of Christ. Christ is the Lamb of God whose sacrifice delivers the faithful from death, as the sacrifice of the Passover Lamb delivered the ancient Jews from slavery and death in Egypt (Ex. 12; 13; 1 Cor. 5:7, 8). (see Pascha).

PASCHAL HOURS - During Bright Week the Hours (as well as certain other services of the Daily Cycle) are replaced by the festive Paschal Hours. The Paschal Hours are intended to reflect the joy and celebration of Pascha. The hymnography and prayers center on Christ's victory over sin and death and our hope for salvation.

Paschal week. (Gr. *Diakaimsimos* or "bright week"). The week following the Sunday of Pascha (*Pascha*), signifying the spiritual renewal and joy brought to the world by the resurrected Christ. See BRIGHT WEEK

Paschalion. The table of dates for Pascha and all movable feasts of the year.

PASSION (1) A term used to describe the sacrifice of Christ on the Cross. (2) Holy Week is often called Passion Week, describing Christ's struggle and suffering in Jerusalem. (3) Passions are human appetites or urges—such as hunger, the desire for pleasure and sexual drives—which become a source of sin when not controlled or directed by submission to the will of God (Rom. 1:26; 7:5; Gal. 5:24; Col. 3:5).

PASSION WEEK - The week preceding Pascha, each day commemorates the suffering of our Lord. Thursday evening at Matins the twelve Passion Gospels are read. See HOLY WEEK

Pastoral theology. The theological field that studies the ways and methods to be used by the clergy for carrying through their duties as Pastors of the Church.

Paten. (Gr. *Diskos*). A small round and flat plate made of gold or silver on which the priest places the particles of bread at the celebration of the Eucharist.

Patriarch. (Gr. "in charge of the family"). The highest prelate in the Orthodox Church. Today, there are eight Orthodox prelates called patriarchs.

Patriarchate. An ecclesiastical jurisdiction governed by a patriarch. There are eight such jurisdictions today in the Orthodox Church, the four ancient Patriarchates of the East, and the four Slavic patriarchates.

Patristics. The theological field that studies the lives and the writings of the Fathers of the Church.

Patron Saint. (Gr. *Poliouchos*; Sl. *Nebesny Pokrovitel*). A saint chosen by a group, nation, or organization to be their special advocate, guardian, and protector. The Patron Saint of an individual is usually the saint after whom the individual is named.

PATRONAL FEAST - Patronal feast of a temple is the celebration honoring the feast or saint in whose name the temple is dedicated. "Temple saint" or "saint of the temple" is the patron saint of a temple which bears the name of a saint. Usually a "temple saint" is accorded the same rank of liturgical celebration as a "vigil saint," that is, a saint having a vigil.

PEACE (Heb. shalom) Tranquillity, harmony with God, self, and other people made possible through Christ, who unites human beings to God and to each other. See Rom. 14:17; Gal. 5:22; Eph. 2:13-16; Phil. 4:6, 7.

Pectoral Cross. Worn by Priests, it symbolizes the reality that the priest is the representative of Christ Crucified to the people and to the world, and as Christ's ambassador, he is to bring them the Gospel of the Kingdom. This is an Award given in the Greek Church and has many steps of progreession in the Russian Church i.e. Silver, Gold, & Jeweled.

Pedalion. The book containing the rules and regulations prescribed by the Ecumenical Synods and the Fathers. It is the Constitution of the Orthodox Church.(see Rudder).

PELAGIANISM – The name of a heresy saying that man can save himself without divine grace.

PENANCE, Sacrament of - (Sl. Pokayaniye) Properly the Sacrament of Penitence. A Sacrament by which sins are forgiven when the penitent acknowledges and confesses his sins and receives absolution. See CONFESSION

PENTARCHY - The Pentarchy consisted of the five ancient patriarchates of the undivided Church of the first millennium of her history, including the Churches of Rome, Constantinople, Alexandria, Antioch, and Jerusalem.

Pentecost. (Gr. "fiftieth Day"). A feast celebrated fifty days after Pascha, commemorating the descent of the Holy Spirit onto the disciples of Christ. It is considered to be the birthday of Christianity. Originally an OT harvest festival celebrated fifty days following the Passover. In time, Pentecost became the commemoration of the giving of the Law to Moses on Mt. Sinai. Pentecost took on a new meaning with the descent of the Holy Spirit on the apostles at Pentecost. Through the Sacrament of Chrismation, Orthodox Christians experience their own personal Pentecost. Every Divine Liturgy becomes a Pentecost through the descent of the Holy Spirit on the faithful and the gifts (the bread and wine), transforming them into the Body and Blood of Christ. See Ex. 23:14-17; Lev. 23:15 21; Acts 2:1 41.

Pentecostarion. A liturgical book containing all the prayers, hymns, and services performed during the period of fifty days between the feasts of Pascha and Pentecost.

PENITENTIAL PSALM - The 50th Psalm of David: "Have mercy on me, O God." (English version Psalm 51).

PERICOPE - a portion of text selected to be read aloud, such as the Epistle and Gospel readings. Lectionaries of Scripture, such as the Apostol, are composed of pericopes

which are to be read for the liturgical services of each day.
See LECTIONARY

PERSON (Gr. prosopon; Lat. persona) Regarding the Holy
Trinity, there are three Divine Persons: God the Father,
Son, and Holy Spirit. The Person of God the Son became
Man, Jesus Christ, "for us and for our salvation" (Matt.
28:19). See also HYPOSTASIS.

PETITION - The most widespread form of prayer is
petition, offered in acknowledgment of our weaknesses,
infirmities, and lack of experience. Because of sins and
passions, our souls become weak and sick. Therefore, it is
essential in prayer to ask God to forgive us and help us to
overcome our faults. Sometimes requests are made because
of an impending danger hanging over us, a need, etc.
Petition in prayer is inevitable in view of our weakness and
is readily accepted by the all-merciful Lord (Matt. 7:7; John
16:23).

PHARISEES One of the parties of first-century Judaism.
The Pharisees favored strict legalistic application of
traditional interpretations of the Law stemming from oral
Jewish traditions. Unlike the Sadducees, they believed in
angels and in the resurrection of the dead. The Pharisees
were generally hostile to the mission of Christ, who
condemned their excessive legalism and their
preoccupation with outward forms, ignoring true
righteousness of the heart. See Matt. 3:7; 12:14; 22:34;
23:13-36. See also SADDUCEES.

Phelonion. The topmost and chief vestment of a priest. It
is of brocade or other material, reaching nearly to the
ground at the back and sides, and short, just to cover the
breast in the front. The bishop wears the sakkos instead.
See Chasuble

PHILOKALIA - The Philokalia is a collection of writings,
mostly centering on practicing the virtues and spiritual
living in a monastery. In recent decades it has become an
important resource for Orthodox Christians, laity and clergy
alike, in personal living and in some ways has achieved

status as a major secondary spiritual written resource, after Holy Scripture, along with St. John Climacus' The Ladder of Divine Ascent.

PILGRIM One who makes a journey to a religious shrine or a spiritual journey from sin and suffering in this life to eternal life with Christ in heaven. See Ps. 42:4; Heb. 11:13; 1 Pet. 2:11.

PILGRIMAGES - Journeys to holy places undertaken from motives of devotion to obtain divine help or as acts of penance or thanksgiving.

Polychronion. (Gr. "for many years"). A prayer sung by the chanter or choir in honor of the celebrant bishop or presbyter. Its full version is: "for many years of life" (Gr. *Eis Polla Eti Despota*; Sl. *Mnogaya Lyeta*).

Polyeleos. (Gr. "oil candelabrum"; "abundance of oil and grace").

1.Special hymns sung during the Service of Matins.

2.The great candelabra hanging from the ceiling of an Orthodox church.

3.A descriptive adjective used to describe Christ as the God of Mercy.

POWER (1) A divine attribute or energy (Matt. 6:13; Luke 1:35; Rom. 1:16). (2) The authority and ability to act (Matt. 9:6). (3) A category of angelic beings (Eph. 1:21).

PRAISE To glorify and give thanks to God or to speak highly of someone or something (Judg. 5:3; Ps. 9:1-14; Rom. 15:11).

PRAYER Communion with God through words of praise, thanksgiving, repentance, supplication, and intercession. Prayer is "raising up the heart and mind to God" (St. John of Damascus). Usually prayer is verbal. However, prayer of the heart or in the Spirit, the highest form of prayer, is without words. See Matt. 6:5-13; 21:22; Rom. 8:26; Phil. 4:6; 1 Thess. 5:17.

Presbyter. (Gr. "elder"). now generally called "priest." Presbyter is one of the three orders of the ordained ministry of the Church: bishop, presbyter, and deacon (see 1 Tim.; Acts 14:23; 15:4 23; 1 Tim. 5:17-19; Titus 1:5). Priest are awarded title for length of service and made Archpriest or Protopresbyter.

Presbytera. (Gr.; Sl. *Matushka*). An honorary title for the priest's wife or mother.

PRESANCTIFIED, LITURGY OF - A Liturgy at which there is no consecration, the Bread being consecrated at a previous Liturgy is used for Communion. The Liturgy of the Presanctified is used on Wednesdays and Fridays during Great Lent. It begins with a Vesper service; there is no Epistle or Gospel unless it is a feast day. See LITURGY

Priest. See PRESBYTER

PRIMATE - The title of the ruling archbishop. He exercises jurisdiction over the bishops of a district or country. Usually, primate refers to the first hierarch of an autocephalous or autonomous Orthodox Church. Less often, it is used to refer to the ruling bishop of an archdiocese or diocese.

PRINCIPALITY. A category of angelic beings. The principalities are named thus because they have command over the lower angels, directing them to the fulfilment of divine orders. The management of the universe and the keeping of all the kingdoms and princedoms, of lands and all peoples, races and nations, is also entrusted to them since each kingdom, race, and people have for themselves a special deeper and manager from the heavenly order called the principalities, for all their country. Further, the service of this angelic order (according to the explanation of St. Gregory the Dialogist) consists in teaching the people to requite each person in authority according to his calling. Finally, the angels of this order raise worthy people to various honorable offices and direct them so that they take power not for the sake of their own gain and benefit, nor for the sake of love of honr and vain renown, but for the sake of honor from God, for the sake of spreading and augmenting of His holy glory, and for the sake of the benefit of their neighbors - as serving the general needs of all their subordinates. See ANGEL

PROCEED To come forth from or come to. The Holy Spirit proceeds from the Father, the fountainhead of the Holy Trinity (John 15:26).

PROCESSION OF THE CROSS - A solemn procession of clergy and laity, at the head of which is carried the Holy Cross, banners, icons, etc.? The Procession of the Cross always occur at the end of the Matins of Holy Saturday (the "Burial of Christ") and on the Holy Pascha (Resurrection) at the beginning of the Paschal Midnight Service; besides those occasions, they are held on parish feast-days and on other solemn occasions, as determined by the priest-in-charge.

PROFANE - Not holy. The word can also be used as a verb meaning "to treat something sacred with irreverence."

Prokeimenon. (Gr. "gradual introduction"). A liturgical verse or scriptural passage sung or read before the reading of the Epistle. It serves as an introduction to the theme of this particular reading.

PROPHET One who proclaims the will of God and/or who foretells the future, especially the coming and mission of Christ, through the inspiration of the Holy Spirit. See Deut. 18:18; Acts 28:25.

PROPITIATION An offering that results in atonement, redemption, and reconciliation. Christ offered Himself on the Cross as a propitiation for our sins, to liberate humanity from sin and death. See Rom. 3:21-26; Heb. 2:17; 1 John 2:2; 4:10.

PROSELYTE Literally, "one who comes toward." A proselyte is a convert to the Faith, usually from another religion. In the New Testament, the word usually refers to a Gentile convert to Judaism (see Acts 2:10; 13:43).

Proskomide or Proskomedia. (Gr. "gathering of gifts" or "preparing to receive the gifts"; Sl. *Shertvennik*). The Service of the preparation of the elements of bread and wine before the Liturgy. It takes place on the Table of Oblation (*Prothesis*), which is situated at the left (north) side of the altar.

Prosphoro or Prosphora. (Gr. "offering gift, an item dedicated to God and offered as a votive," also *prosphora*). The altar bread which is leavened and prepared with pure wheat flour to be used for the Eucharist. It is round and stamped on the top with a special seal (*sphragis* or *Panagiari*). It is made in two layers symbolizing the two natures of Christ (Human and Divine). The inscribed parts of the top are used for the Eucharist, and the rest of it is cut into small pieces to be distributed to the faithful (antidoron). In Slavic Churches they often use 5 smaller loaves for this service.

PROSTRATION - A posture of humility or adoration when in prayer one kneels and bows the head to the floor.

PROTECTION OF THE MOTHER OF GOD - The Protection of the Mother of God is one of the most beloved feast days on the Orthodox calendar among the Slavic peoples, commemorated on October 1. The feast is celebrated additionally on October 28 in the Greek tradition. It is also known as the feast of the Virgin Mary's Cerement.

PROTHESIS - The Greek word used (1) for the table (zhertvennik) on which the preparation of the elements for Divine Liturgy is made; (2) for the Proskomedia itself. See PROSKOMIDE

PROTOMARTYR - One of the various customary saint titles used in commemoration at divine services when remembering saints on the Church Calendar. - The first martyr in a given region (in the case of St. Stephen (ACTS 7:60) , the first martyr of the whole Church).

PROTOPRESBYTER - A title of honor given by the Council of Bishops to an archpriest for long or outstanding service to the Church. See PRESBYTER

PROVIDENCE God's sovereign care in governing His creation, especially His care for the faithful (Rom. 8:28).

PSALM - An ancient Hebraic hymn that has, in various instances, a doxological, penitential, didactic, or messianic content. In many respects, psalms served as models for the composition of new Christian hymns, and also came to be incorporated as important elements into all forms of the Christian liturgy.

Psalter. The Psalter contains the 150 Psalms of David, divided into twenty Kathismas, as well as the text of the Nine Biblical Canticles sung at Matins.

Pulpit. See AMBON.

PURIFICATION The Old Testament rite whereby one is cleansed of ritual impurity caused by such things as contact with leprosy or a dead body, or sexual functions. This cleansing consisted of making a sacrifice or being sprinkled with "water of purification" (Num. 19:9). Christ liberated the faithful from these rites. Christians are purified by the sacraments and by their spiritual struggle towards transforming their passions. See Lev. 12:6; Num. 19:9 21; Matt. 15:11; Luke 2:22-33; Acts 10:9-16; 15:1-29.

PYX – Artopharion. The box or vessel in which the Reserved Sacraments are kept in the Tabernacle, and also the box which is used for carrying the Reserved Sacraments to give communion to the sick.

-R-

RADONITSA - ("Day of Rejoicing", Krasnaya Gorka) is a holiday in the Orthodox Church which falls on the Monday or (more commonly) Tuesday of Saint Thomas Week - eight or nine days, respectively, after Pascha (Pascha). The day is a general memorial for the departed.

RAPTURE The gathering of the Church on earth in the presence of Christ when He comes again to judge the living and the dead (1 Thess. 4:15-17). Orthodox theologians reject the recent sectarian view that the Church will be taken out of the world before the time of trouble preceding the Second Coming. Christ specifically teaches the faithful will experience the trials of tribulation (Matt. 24:>28). See also SECOND COMING.

Raso. (see cassock).

Reader. (Gr. *Anagnostis*, Sl. *Chtets*). The individual assigned to read, chant, and give responses in church services. Usually, such a person will be blessed by the bishop with special prayers and in a special ceremony.

RECONCILIATION The removal of hostility and barriers between humans and God, and between individuals, accomplished by Christ (Rom. 5:11; 2 Cor. 5:18, 19).

RECTOR - (Lat. to guide, govern) A priest who is in charge of a parish and hence ex-officio head of all its organizations. He is the presiding officer at all Parish meetings, Supervisor of the Church School. These offices he may delegate to others. All work that may be done in the Parish is done with regard to his consent and approval.

REDEMPTION The deliverance of humanity from sin and death by Christ, who assumed humanity by His Incarnation, conquered sin and death by His life-giving death and glorious Resurrection, releases those who are in captivity to the evil one, and unites humanity to God by His Ascension (Gal. 3:13; Heb. 9:15). See also DEIFICATION and SALVATION.

Relics. (Gr. *Leipsana Agia*). The remains from the body of a Saint or even a Saint's possessions, such as clothes or vestments. The relics are honored and venerated by all Orthodox. Upon the consecration of a new church, the consecrating bishop embeds holy relics in the Altar Table, following the ancient traditions of the church in performing the Eucharist on the tombs of Martyrs (*Martyria*).

REMEMBRANCE (Gr. anamnesis) Making present by means of recollection. The Eucharist is not merely a calling to mind but a remembrance of and mystical participation in the very sacrifice of Christ, His Resurrection, His Ascension, and His coming again (1 Cor. 11:23 26).

REMISSION The forgiveness and putting aside of sins. As the faithful are released from their sins through the sacramental life of the Church, they in turn are called to remit the sins of any who have offended them See John 20:23; Acts 2:37, 38.

REPENTANCE Literally, "a change of mind" or attitude, and thus of behavior. God is the author of repentance, which is an integral part of baptism, confession, and ongoing spiritual life. Repentance is not simply sorrow for sins but a firm determination to turn away from sin to a new life of righteousness in Jesus Christ. See Matt. 4:17; 2 Pet. 3:9; 1 John 1:9.

REQUIEM - (Paneheda, Pannikhida) A service for the repose of the souls of the departed faithful. See MEMORIAL , PARASTAS, PANNIKHIDA

RESURRECTION The reunion of the soul and body after death which will revitalize and transform the physical body into a spiritual body. Jesus Himself is the firstfruits of perfect resurrection; He will never again be subject to death. Because He conquered death by His Resurrection, all will rise again: the righteous to life with Christ, the wicked to judgment. See John 5:28, 29; 1 Cor. 15:35 55.

REVELATION - (1) Making known the hidden things concerning God and His divine truths through God chosen men who put these things in writing which make up the books of the Old and the New Testaments. (2) The last Book of the New Testament, a prophetic book written by St. John the Divine.

REVEREND - (Lat. worthy of respect) A title applied to the clergy. Higher ranks of clergy are "Very," and "Right" for the mitred clergy.

RIGHT REVEREND - The title given to bishops. "Most Reverend" to Archbishops and the Metropolitan.

RIGHT-BELIEVING - One of the various customary saint titles used in commemoration at divine services when remembering saints on the Church Calendar. An epithet used for sainted secular rulers.

RIGHTEOUS - One of the various customary saint titles used in commemoration at divine services when remembering saints on the Church Calendar. A holy person under the Old Covenant (Old Testament Israel) but also sometimes used for married saints of the New Covenant (the Church); righteous may also used as a translation for the Greek hosios, which is usually translated as "venerable."

RIGHTEOUSNESS Being good, just, and blameless. All are called to a life of humble obedience to God. However, acts of righteousness cannot earn salvation. Rather, righteousness is the fruit of the Holy Spirit, and the way in which Christians respond with living faith to God's gift of salvation. See Matt. 5:6, 20; Rom. 4:3; Gal. 5:22; James 2:14-26.

RIPIDION - (Gr. fan) A flat metal disk representing a cherub's head surrounded by six wings mounted upright on a shaft. There are two of them in back of the altar and they are carried at processions.

Rite. (Gr. *Telete*, Sl. *Tchin*). The performance of a religious ceremony following a prescribed order of words and actions (see *typikon*). See Byzantine Rite, Western Rite , Old-Rite.

RITUAL Ceremonies and texts used in the worship of the Church. Having her roots in the temple and synagogue, the Church has employed ritual in her worship from the very beginning. See also LITURGY and WORSHIP.

Royal doors. The Royal Doors are the central doors of the iconostasis, directly in front of the altar in an Orthodox church. On the Doors there is usually a diptych of the Annunciation. Sometimes they may also have the icons of the four evangelists. The Doors are opened at different points during the Divine Liturgy and other liturgical services depending on local tradition. However, they are almost always opened during the Great and Little Entrances, the Gospel reading, and the distribution of the Eucharist.

Royal Hours. On the Eves of the Nativity of Christ and Theophany, as well as on Holy Friday, all of the Hours, as well as the Typical Psalms, are sung as one Service, characterized by special Psalms and hymns, as well as special Old Testament, Epistle and Gospel Readings, relating to the particular Feast or events of that day. In ancient times, it was customary for the Byzantine Emperor to be present for the whole Service, hence the title Royal Hours.

ROYAL PRIESTHOOD - (The Laity) All true believers in the Church. It is the responsibility of all believers for the preservation and propagation of the Gospel and the Church, and to give thanks to God. All were created to bless and praise God, to worship Him. This is the primary human vocation because this is precisely what human beings were created to do: to be in communion with God as His priests, and in that role to worship Him. See LAITY

RUBRICS - (Sl. Typikon) Rules for the conduct of the services of the Church. Canon law requires strict observance of the rubrics in the liturgical books for the celebration of Divine Liturgy and the administration of the Sacraments. See TYPIKON

Rudder. (Gr. *Pedalion*). The book containing the rules and regulations prescribed by the Ecumenical Synods and the Fathers. It is the Constitution of the Orthodox Church.

Rule of Prayer – A daily prayer discipline. Many rules of prayer have developed in the history of the Church. At no place or time has there been a uniform rule. Therefore, the term "Rule of Prayer" should never be understood as a strait jacket, regulating and limiting our communion with God. Those who are fortunate enough to have a spiritual father should consult him before establishing a Rule. Those who do not, should begin with a modest Rule, increasing it only when it has become a regular and integral part their lives.

RYASA - The black cassock worn by the priest or bishop. Usually, it is black, but it may be any other shade or color. It has wide sleeves. Another cassock, with narrow sleeves (podryasnik) is often worn under the ryasa. See CASSOCK

-S-

SABAOTH - "The Lord of Sabaoth." The word taken from the Hebrew, literally, means hosts or powers.

SABBATH - The seventh day of the week, originally a day of rest, for after creation "God rested on the seventh day" (Gen. 2:2). Since Christ rose from the dead on the first day of the week, Sunday, the Church gathers on this day instead of the seventh to worship God. Sunday is also called "the Lord's Day" and "the eighth day," because it transcends the Sabbath and is seen as being a part of heavenly time rather than earthly time. (Ex. 20:8-11; Acts 20:7.)

SABELLIANISM – The name of a heresy saying that the Father, Son and Holy Spirit are only "modes" or "masks" of one divine Person.

Sacrament. (Gr. *Mysterion;* Sl. *Tainstvo*). The outward and visible part of religion, consisting of various ceremonies, words, and symbolisms, producing an invisible action by the Holy Spirit that confers grace on an individual. All Sacraments were instituted by Christ for the salvation of the believer. Orthodox Christians frequently speak of seven sacraments, but God's gift of grace is not limited only to these seven—the entire life of the Church is mystical and sacramental. The sacraments were instituted by Christ Himself (John 1:16, 17). The seven mysteries are baptism (Matt. 28:18-20; Rom. 6:4; Gal. 3:27), chrismation (Acts 8:15-17; 1 John 2:27), the Holy Eucharist (Matt. 26:26 28; John 6:30-58; 1 Cor. 10:16; 11:23-31), confession John 20:22, 23; 1 John 1:8, 9), ordination (Mark 3:14; Acts 1:15-26; 6:1-6; 1 Tim. 3:1-13; 4:14), marriage (Gen. 2:18 25; Eph. 5:22-33), and unction (Luke 9:1 6; James 5:14, 15).

Sacrifice. (Gr. *Thysia*; Sl. *Zhertva*). The bloodless offering to God, which is the Holy Eucharist offered at the Liturgy. It signifies the sacrifice of Christ on the cross for man's salvation. See also REMEMBRANCE.

SACRILEGE - A violation or contemptuous treatment of a person, thing, or place, publicly dedicated to the worship of God. The administering or reception of sacraments in an unworthy manner is a sacrilege.

Sacristy. (Gr. *Skevophylakion*; Sl. *Riznitsa*). A utility room at the right side (south) of the altar, where vestments and sacred vessels are kept and where the clergy vest for services.

SADDUCEES A party in Judaism at the time of Christ. The Sadducees steadfastly held to a literal interpretation of the Law contained in the first five books of the Old Testament (the Pentateuch or Torah), and rejected traditional interpretations favored by other groups of Jews, especially the Pharisees. Sadducees came from the priestly class and rejected the resurrection of the dead and the existence of angels. Christ condemned these Jewish leaders for their preoccupation with outward forms, ignoring or neglecting true righteousness of the heart (Matt. 16:1-12)

Saints. (Gr. *Agios*). All holy men, women, and angels, who, through a pure and holy life on earth or through martyrdom and confession of faith in word and deeds, have merited the canonization of the Church. The saints and the other pious people who are in glory with God constitute the "Triumphant Church."

Sakkos or Dalmatic. The main vestment worn by the bishop during the Liturgy. It originates from the vestments of the Byzantine emperor.

SALVATION The fulfillment of humanity in Christ, through deliverance from the curse of sin and death, to union with God through Christ the Savior. Salvation includes a process of growth of the whole person whereby the sinner is changed into the image and likeness of God. One is saved by faith through grace. However, saving faith is more than mere belief. It must be a living faith manifested by works of righteousness, whereby we cooperate with God to do His will. We receive the grace of God for salvation through participation in the sacramental life of the Church. See articles, "The New Birth," at John 3; "Justification by Faith," at Rom. 5; and "Deification," at 2 Pet. 1; 2 Cor. 3:18; 4:16; 5:17; Eph. 2:8, 9; Phil. 2:12, 13; James 2:14 26; 1 Pet. 2:2. See also DEIFICATION, JUSTIFICATION, REDEMPTION and SACRAMENT.

SANCTIFICATION - 1) Literally, "being set apart" to God. The process of growth in Christ whereby the believer is made holy as God is holy, through the Holy Spirit (2 Pet. 1; Rom. 6:22; Rom. 15:16). See also DEIFICATION, JUSTIFICATION and SALVATION.

Salutations. (see *Akathistos* hymn).

SANCTUARY The Holy of Holies or Most Holy Place—the place in the Old Testament tabernacle or temple containing the ark of the covenant, the dwelling place of God. Only the High Priest could enter the Most Holy Place and only on the Day of Atonement. When the early Christians built churches, they followed the general pattern of the temple, and the altar area is often called the sanctuary. See Ex. 26:31-35; 40:34, 35; Lev. 16:1-5; 1 Kin. 6:1-38; 8:1-11. See Altar.

SATAN - An angelic being hostile to God; the devil. See DEVIL

Schism. Formal separation from the unity of the one true Church. Although the Christian Church has witnessed several schisms, the most disastrous was the separation of the Greek Paschan and the Roman Western Church in 1054, dividing Christendom into two parts.

SEAL - (1) Any stamp or impression of a Cross, especially the central part of the prosphora. (2) The Sign of the Cross made by a Bishop or Priest with the right hand in blessing. (3) The blessing of themselves by the faithful with the Sign of the Cross. See PROSKOMEDE.

SECOND COMING At the end of the ages, Christ will come again to judge the living and the dead. Following the judgment, a new heaven and new earth will take the place of the old earth, which has been scarred by sin. Because Christ is already present through the Church, Christians enter into the Kingdom through their participation in the sacramental life of the Church as they await the coming of the Lord (see, Titus 2; Matt. 25:314 6; Rom. 8:18 21; 1 Thess. 4:16,17; Rev. 20:11 - 22:5). See also RESURRECTION & RAPTURE.

See. (Gr. *Hedra* or *Thronos*). The official "seat" or city capital where a bishop resides (esp. for a large jurisdiction); hence, the territory of his entire jurisdiction may be called his See.

SEMINARY - A school of higher learning exclusively devoted to the training of candidates for the priesthood.

SEPTUAGINT -see LXX

SERAPHIM - A category of angelic beings. The six-winged Seraphim are the angels closest to God (Isaiah 6:2) who, due to their closeness to God, resemble fire (Hebrews 12:29; Daniel 7:9; Exodus 24:17; Psalms 103:4). Due to this closeness to God, and their appearance, they were given the name 'seraphim', which in Hebrew means 'flaming'. They are aflame with love for God and kindle others to such love.

SERMON - A discourse usually based upon a text from the Bible and delivered from the Ambo to give religious instruction, to preach the Word of God, to proclaim the Gospel.

Service books. They are special books containing the hymns or the services of the Orthodox Church. There are eight, as follows: Gospel (*Evangelion*), Book of Epistles (*Apostolos*), Psalter (*Octoechos* or *paraklitiki*), *Triodion, Pentecostarion*, Twelve *Menaia, Horologion*, and Service or Liturgy book (*Euchologio* or *Ieratiko*).

Service Book or Ieratikon or Litourgikon or Euchologio. (Sl. *Sluzhebnik*). The liturgical book containing the prayers and ceremonial order of the various church services including the Liturgy.

SEXTON - A layman whose duty is to keep the church building clean, ring the bells and other duties under the direction of the rector.

Sign of the Cross. The Orthodox make the Sign of the Cross to signify their belief in the sacrifice of Christ upon the cross for man's salvation. It is made by the right hand in a cruciform gesture touching the forehead, chest, right and left shoulders with the tips of fingers (the thumb, index, and middle finger joined together as a symbol of the Holy Trinity, the ring and little fingers touching the palm as a symbol of the two Natures of Christ).

SHEKINAH - The glory of God, frequently revealed in the symbols of fire and cloud in the Old Testament. Although Christians experience the energies of God, including His glory, they never penetrate beyond the cloud to the inner essence of God, which remains hidden. (Ex. 13:21; 24:15 18; 33:18-23; 40:34, 35; 2 Chr. 7:1; Matt. 17:1-5.)? See also ENERGY and ESSENCE.

SIN (Gr. hamartia) Literally, "missing the mark." This word in ancient Greek could describe the action of an archer who failed to hit the target. All humans are sinners who miss the mark of perfection that God has set for His people, resulting in alienation from God, sinful actions that violate the law of God, and ultimately in death. See Matt. 5:48; Rom. 3:23; 6:23; 1 John 1:8.

SIX PSALMS - (*Hexapsalmos*) The suite of six psalms read at the start of Matins: Psalms 3, 37 (38), 62 (63), 87 (88), 102 (103), and 142 (143). Matins begins with the reading of the "Six Psalms," i.e. Psalms 3, 37, 62, 87, 102, and 142, read in that order, and combined into a single whole.

SECT. See CULT

SKETE. Typically, a secluded monastic community with a small chapel surrounded by monastic kellia or cells where the monks lived and did their private prayer rule or cell rule, and some handiwork. A spiritual father or abbot guided the spiritual endeavors of the monks of this community. See KELLIA

SKUFIA - (Sl.) A head covering worn by a priest, given by the Bishop as an award for faithful service.

SLAVA - The slava, also called krsna slava and krsno ime (literally 'christened name' in Serbian), is the Orthodox Christian tradition of the ritual celebration, veneration and observance of a family's own patron saint. The family celebrates the slava annually on the patron saint's feast day. The slava is primarily associated with the Serbs; they regard it as one of their most significant holidays.

SOJOURNER A stranger or foreigner. Because the Church exists in a sinful world that has rejected God, Christians citizens of the Kingdom of God—are strangers in a foreign land. Therefore, faithful sojourners are on guard, lest they adopt the ways of the fallen society in which they live. See 1 Pet. 2:11; 1 John 2:1 917.

Solea. An area with elevated floor in front of the iconostasis of the church, where the various rites and church ceremonies are held.

SON OF MAN An important messianic title of Christ, who is perfect God and perfect Man. The Gospels reveal that

Jesus often applied this title to Himself. In Christ, the Second Adam, God assumed and perfected sinful humanity, freeing those who follow Him from the consequences of the rebellion of the first man, Adam. See Mark 2:28; 9:31; Rom. 5:12-21; 1 Cor. 15:21, 22, 45-49. See also INCARNATION

SORROW Sadness and grief caused by the realization of one's sins. The Scriptures distinguish between godly sorrow, which produces repentance, and ungodly sorrow, the sadness of being found out, which produces death (Matt. 5:4; 2 Cor. 7:9, 10). Christ has conquered suffering and death, the cause of sadness, and turns true sorrow to joy for His followers (John 16:20-22, 33).

Soteriology. Theological field studying the mission and work of Christ as Redeemer (*Soter*).

SOUL A living substance, simple, bodiless, and invisible by nature, activating the body to which it brings life, growth, sensation and reproduction. The mind is not distinct from the soul but serves as a window to the soul. The soul is free, endowed with will, and the power to act. Along with the body, the soul is created by God in His image. The soul of man will never die (Gen. 1:26; 2:7; Matt. 10:28).

Sphragis. (see *prosphoro*).

SPIRITUALITY The ascetic and pious struggle against sin through repentance, prayer, fasting, and participation in the sacramental life of the Church. See Gal. 5:16 26; Phil. 2:12, 13. See also SYNERGISM.

Spiritual Father. See Startez & Confessor

Spiritual relationship. (see affinity).

Spoon. Usually silver or gold on top of which is a cross, it is used to receive the Holy Blood with.

STARETZ - A staretz (Russian) or geronta (Gr, pronounced yeronda, both literally meaning elder) is a holy person gifted with the charism of spiritual direction, often a monk or hermit (not necessarily a priest), in the Church. The plural of the Russian form is startsy.

STAUROPIGION - A monastery directly subject to a Patriarch.

STAVOPEGIAL - A stavropegial (stavropigial or stavropighial) institution, usually a monastery, is one which falls directly under the omophorion of the primate of a church rather than under the local diocesan bishop.

Stichar. (see Alb).

Stikheron (Stikhera). A Stikheron is a stanza sung between verses taken from the Psalms, primarily at Vespers (at Lord, I have called... and the Apostikha) and Matins (at the Apostikha).

STEWARD(SHIP) A steward is one who manages property belonging to another. All a Christian has belongs to God. Thus, the Christian gives back to God out of the material blessings he has received from God for the work of the Church. In the Old Testament God commanded the faithful to give ten percent of their goods to God; though not under law, Christians should give at least as much. Christians are also stewards of the spiritual knowledge which God has entrusted to us. We must preserve the heritage of apostolic doctrine intact for future generations. See Gen. 14:18-20; Lev. 27:30 33; 1 Cor. 4:1, 2; 2 Cor. 9:6 8; 1 Pet. 4:10.

SYMBOL In Orthodox usage, the manifestation in material form of a spiritual reality. A symbol does not merely stand for something else, as does a "sign'; it indicates the actual presence of its subject. For example, the dove is the symbol which brought to Jesus the descent of the Holy Spirit (Matt. 3:13-16).

Subdeacon. (Gr. *hypodiakonos*).An assistant or a server at the services of a bishop; vesting the bishop and handing him the dikerion and trikerion.

SYNAPTES - Petitions that refer either to the Great or Little Ektenia (Litany). See EKTENIA or LITANY

Synaxarion.

1.A brief biography of a saint read in the church on occasions of his feast day.

2.Book or books containing lives of the saints.

Synaxis. (Gr. "assembly"; Sl. *Sobor*). A gathering of the faithful in honor of a saint or for reading passages from his biography (*synaxarion*). The first part of the Divine Liturgy is called the synaxis because the faithful gather to sing, to hear the Scriptures read, and to hear the homily. The saints' days are also called a synaxis, such as the Synaxis of St. Michael and all the angels.

SYNERGISM (from Gr. syn: same, together; ergos: energy, work) Working together, the act of cooperation. In referring to the New Testament, synergism is the idea of being "workers together with" God (2 Cor. 6:1), or of working "out your own salvation . . . for it is God who works in you" (Phil. 2:12, 13). This is not a cooperation between "equals," but finite man working together with Almighty God. Nor does synergism suggest working for, or earning, salvation. God offers salvation by His grace, and man's ability to cooperate also is a grace. Therefore, man responds to salvation through cooperation with God's grace in living faith, righteous works and rejection of evil (James 2:14-26). See also FREE WILL and PASSIONS.

Synod. (see Ecumenical Council).

SYNOPTIC (from Gr. syn: same, together; optic: eye, vision) The books of Matthew, Mark, and Luke, which hold essentially the same viewpoint and "look alike," are called the synoptic Gospels.

-T-

Tabernacle. (Gr. *Artophorion*;   Sl. *Darochranitelnitsa*). An elaborate ark or receptacle kept on the Altar Table, in which the Holy Gifts of the Eucharist are preserved for the communion of the sick or for the Liturgy of the Presanctified Gifts during Lent.

TEMPLE - 1) refers to the building in which the Church worships. 2) (an appellation of the Theotokos) The Prophet Ezekiel speaks of the Temple whose East gate remains sealed, through which only the Lord, the God of Israel, has entered. This clearly prophesies the Virgin Birth of the Theotokos (Ez. 44:1-2).

TEMPTATION The seductive attraction of sin. Christ was tempted by Satan and has overcome the power of temptation. Those united to Christ are given His power also to withstand the temptation of sin through patience, courage, and obedience. See Matt. 4:1-11; 1 Cor. 10:13; Heb. 2:17, 18; James 1:12.

TETRAPOD - (Gr. artophorion) A square table placed in the center of the church with an icon of the Feast Day or the Patron Saint for veneration.

THANKSGIVING To be grateful, to offer thanks, especially to God for His love and mercy. The Eucharistic prayer is called the thanksgiving (see 1 Thess. 5:18).

Thaumatourgos. (Gr.   "miracle-worker"; Sl. *Chudotvorets*). A title given to some saints distinguished among the faithful for their miracles.

THEOLOGIAN - Theology deals with God, our participation in Him, and the underlying divine reality inherent in creation. It is far more than intellectual and scholarly discourse about God, and is not acquired through academic study.

THEOPHANY A manifestation of God in His uncreated glory. It refers also to Christ's resurrection appearances. The revelation of the Holy Trinity at the Baptism of Christ (Luke 3:21, 22) is the greatest theophany; it is celebrated in the Orthodox Church on Epiphany (Jan. 6). Other theophanies are found throughout the Bible. For example, God appeared to Abraham in the form of three men (Gen.

18:1-15), and to Jacob in a dream (Gen. 28:10 17). See also EPIPHANY.

THEOSIS. is the acquisition of the Holy Spirit, whereby through Grace one becomes a participant in the Kingdom of God. Theosis literally means to become gods by Grace. The Biblical words that are synonymous and descriptive of Theosis are: adoption, edemption, inheritance, glorification, holiness and perfection. Theosis is an act of the uncreated and infinite love of God. It begins here in time and space, but it is not static or complete, and is an open ended progression uninterrupted through all eternity. See DEIFICATION

Theotokos. A theological term commonly used by the Orthodox to indicate the doctrinal significance of Virgin Mary as Mother of God. God-bearer, birth-giver, frequently translated "Mother of God." Because Jesus Christ is the divine Son of God, Mary is called the Mother of God to profess our faith that in the Incarnation, God was in her womb. Elizabeth called Mary "blessed" and "the mother of my Lord" (Luke 1:42, 43). At the Council of Ephesus in A.D. 431, the Church condemned Nestorius and other heretics who refused to call the Virgin Mary the Theotokos. For if it was not God in Mary's womb, there is no salvation for humanity.

Theotokion. (Gr. "referring to *Theotokos*"; Sl. *Bogorodichey*). These are Troparia or Stikhera sung in honor of the Theotokos. On Wednesdays and Fridays, these Theotokia usually take the theme of the Theotokos at the Lord's Crucifixion, and thus are called Cross-Theotokia (or Stavro-Theotokia).

Three hierarchs. The Orthodox Church considers in particular three bishops (hierarchs) of the Church as Her most important Teachers and Fathers, who contributed to the development and the spiritual growth of the Church. They are St. Basil the Great, St. Gregory the Theologian, and St. John Chrysostom. Their feast day is observed on January 30, a day also dedicated to Hellenic letters since the three hierarchs contributed to the development of Greek Christian education and literature.

THRONE A category of angelic beings. Thereafter the seraphim and cherubim stand the God-bearing thrones (as St. Dionysius the Areopagite calls them) before Him Who sits on the high and exulted throne, being named "thrones" since on them, as on intellectual thrones (as writes St. Maximus the Confessor) God intellectually resides. Residing on them in an incomprehensible manner, God makes His righteous judgement, according to the word of David: "Thou hast sat upon a throne, O Thou that judgest righteousness" (Ps 9:4). Therefore through them the justice of God is pre-eminently manifested; they serve His justice, glorifying it and pouring out the power of justice onto the thrones of earthly judges, helping kings and masters to bring forth right judgement.

TITHES - (Sl. Desyatina) The tenth part, held from the earliest times to be due to God. (GEN. 14:20; LEV. 27:30; HEB. 7:5). Payment is the recognized fulfillment of the natural obligation of the faithful to contribute to the support of the clergy and the Church.

Titular bishop. An auxiliary bishop without his own territorial or residential diocese, who is usually assisting a senior bishop with a large jurisdiction (Archbishop or Patriarch). The episcopal title of a titular bishop is sometimes taken from an ancient diocese which once flourished but now exists only in name, and, therefore, a titular bishop does not have his own jurisdiction.

TOMOS - small book that contains a major announcement or similar text promulgated by a Holy Synod, such as a grant of autocephaly.

TONE - The standard melody for versicles, tro-parions and prokimenons is arranged into Eight Tones, which are sung in a continuous cycle throughout the year. See EIGHT TONES

TONSURE - The tonsure, which is the cutting of hair from the head in the sign of the cross, is the sign that the person completely offers himself to God -- hair being the symbol of strength (Jud 16:17).

TRADITION (Gr. *Paradosis*) That which is handed down, the transmission of the doctrine or the customs of the Orthodox Church through the centuries, basically by word of mouth from generation to generation.. Tradition is the life of the Church in the Holy Spirit, for the Holy Spirit leads the Church "into all truth" (John 16:13) and enables her to preserve the truth taught by Christ to His Apostles. The Holy Scriptures are the core of Holy Tradition, as interpreted through the writings of the Fathers, the Ecumenical Councils, and the worship of the Church. Together, these traditions manifest the faith of the ancient undivided Church, inspired by the Holy Spirit to preserve the fullness of the gospel. See John 21:25; Acts 15:1-29; 2 Thess. 2:15.

Transfiguration. (Gr. *Metamorphosis*).   The transfiguration of Christ is a major feast day (August 6) commemorating the appearance of Christ in divine glory along with Moses and the prophet Elias on Mount Tabor (cf. Matt. 17: 1-7). Christians are called to be transformed by the Holy Spirit into the image and likeness of God (Rom. 12:1, 2). See also DEIFICATION.

TRIBULATION (THE) - The Scriptures reveal that much trouble and violence "Great Tribulation" will engulf the world before the Second Coming of Christ (Matt. 24:4-29). See also ESCHATOLOGY, RAPTURE, and SECOND COMING.

TRINITY - God the Father and His Son and His Holy Spirit: one in essence and undivided. God revealed the mystery of the Trinity at Christ's baptism (Matt. 3:13 17), but even before that event, numerous Old Testament references pointed to the Trinity. For example, the frequent use of plural pronouns referring to the one God (Gen. 1:26); the three angels who appeared to Abraham (Gen. 18:1-16);

and the Triple Holy hymn sung by the angels in Isaiah's vision (Is. 6:1 4) all suggest one God in three Persons, the Father, Son, and Holy Spirit (Matt. 28:19).

Triodion. (Gr. "three odes or modes").

   1.The period between the Sunday of the Pharisee and the Publican, and Cheese-Fare Sunday.

   2.A Liturgical book containing the hymns, prayers, and services of the movable feast before Pascha, beginning with the Sunday of the Pharisee and the Publican and lasting until Pascha Sunday.

Trisagion. (Gr. "thrice-holy"). The biblical Trisagion, "Holy, Holy, Holy," is the hymn of the angels before the throne of God (Is. 6:1-3; Rev. 4:8).

   1.One of the most ancient hymns of the church, used by the Orthodox in every prayer or service: "Holy God, Holy Mighty, Holy Immortal, have mercy upon us."

   2.In Greek usage it is also known as a memorial Service performed by the graveside or in church for the repose of the soul. In Slavic usage it is called a *Litya*.

Troparion. This is simply a short musical composition similar in length and style to the Kontakion. They are sung at the end of Vespers, after God is the Lord... and the Apostikha at Matins, at the Liturgy and other services.

TYPE A historical event that has a deeper meaning, pointing to our salvation in Christ. For example, the three days that Jonah spent in the belly of the fish is a type of the three days that Christ would spend in the tomb (Matt. 12:40). The serpent that Moses lifted up on the staff is a type of the lifting up of Christ on the Cross (John 3:14-16). The burning bush, aflame but not consumed, is a type of the Virgin Mary, who carried the incarnate God in her womb but was not consumed by His presence (Luke 1:2638). Noah's ark, which saved Noah and his family from death in the flood, is a type of baptism, which brings the believer from death to life (1 Pet. 3:18-22). See also ALLEGORY.

TYPIKA - The Typika (Reader's Service) is a brief service that is appointed by the Typikon for certain occasions but may also be conducted when a priest or bishop is not present.

TYPICAL PSALMS - The Typical Psalms are Psalms 102 (103) and 145 (146), which may be included in either the Divine Liturgy (in Slavic practice, and in Byzantine monastic practice) or the Typika. In the context of the liturgy, these Psalms form the first two antiphons along with Saint Justinian's Hymn. The third antiphon (which is also included in the Typika) is the Beatitudes. See ANTIPHON

Typikon. (Gr. "following the order"; Sl. *Sluzhebnik*). Liturgical book which contains instructions about the order of the various church services and ceremonies in the form of a perpetual calendar. According to Church Tradition, the Typikon was drawn up by St. Sabbas of Jerusalem (532) and later revised by St. Sophronius, Patriarch of Jerusalem (638). A further revision was made by St. John of Damascus (749), a Monk at St. Sabbas' Monastery, hence the name the Jerusalem Typikon of St. Sabbas' Monastery. In 1888, a new edition of the Typikon was prepared at Constantinople, which, in modern times, is used primarily by the Greek-speaking Churches. The Church of Russia, as well as, for the most part, still adheres to the Jerusalem Typikon, as do the older Greek monasteries, such as those of Mt. Athos, St. Sabbas at Jerusalem, and St. John on Patmos.

-U-

Unction. Anointing of the sick with blessed oil, for the healing of body and soul. The gift of healing is bestowed by the Holy Spirit through the anointing, together with the prayers of the Unction service. (James 5:14, 15; 1 John 2:20.) The seventh Sacrament of Unction with Oil is a special ceremony of anointing the sick for healing the ailments of the body and the soul. This ceremony is usually performed at the bedside of the sick. The ceremony calls for seven priests and seven Gospels and Epistles are read. This Sacrament was instituted by our Lord and practiced in Apostolic times. See also SACRAMENT

UNFROCK – "Defrock" To deprive a priest or bishop of his Orders for a grave offense.

Uniate. The Churches of Paschan Christendom in communion with Rome, which yet retain their respective languages, rites, and canon law in accordance with the terms of their union. The term 'Uniate' (Polish Unia) was first used by the opponents of the Union of Brest-Litovsk (1595). Today these churches are called Roman Catholic of the Byzantine Rite. (see Byzantine Rite).

Unleavened bread. Bread baked without yeast. The Jews used unleavened bread for the Passover to symbolize the fact that they had no time to wait for the yeast to rise in the bread (Ex. 12:1-20). By contrast, the bread of the New Covenant is leavened. See also LEAVENED.

UNMERCENARY - One of the various customary saint titles used in commemoration at divine services when remembering saints on the Church Calendar. saint who refused to take payment for heal

---

-V-

VAINGLORY - Elation or pride over one's own achievements, abilities, etc.; boastful vanity.

VEIL - (Sl. Vozduh) Covering for the chalice and paten used at the service of Divine Liturgy.

VENERATION - The respect and honor given to the saints. The veneration which is given to the Most-Holy

Virgin and the saints is different from the worship given to God alone.

Vespers. (Gr. *Esperinos*;). An important service of the Orthodox Church, held in the evening, which is mainly a Thanksgiving prayer for the closing day and a welcome of the new one to come the following morning. On the eve of an important holiday, the Vesper Service includes *Artoklasia* or the blessing of the five loaves (Gr. *artos*; Sl. *Litiya*) for health and the well-being of the faithful.

VESSELS, SACRED - The chalice, paten, spoon and spear (these are also called the Eucharistic vessels). These are not handled by laymen.

Vestments. (Gr. *Amphia*). The distinctive garments worn by the clergy in the liturgy and the other church services, See also: Epigonation, Epitrachelion, Omophorion, Orarion, Rason, Sakkos, Sticharion, Zone.

Vicar Bishop. See Titular bishop.

Vigil. (Gr. *olonychtia*). Spiritual exercises during the night preceding the feast day of a saint or another major feast, observed by various spiritual preparations, prayers, and services. See All-Night Vigil

VIRTUE - A righteous characteristic such as self-control, patience, or humility; the opposite of vice or passion. As a person grows spiritually, he or she grows in virtue while the passions are conquered by the grace of God. (Phil. 4:8; 2 Pet. 1:2-7.) See also PASSION, VIRTUES

Virtues. Fruits of the Spirit (Galatians 5:22-23) 1.Love, 2. Joy, 3. Peace, 4. Patience (Long-suffering), 5. Kindness, 6. Goodness, 7. Faithfulness, 8. Modesty, 9. Self Control

VLADIKA - When speaking with a Bishop, you should say "Bless, Despota [Thés-po-ta]" (or "Vladika [Vlá-dee-ka]" in Slavonic, "Master" in English). It is also appropriate to say, "Bless, Your Grace" (or "Your Eminence," etc.). You should end your conversation by asking for a blessing again. This is in respect to the bishop's teaching ministry (ie, a school master).

VOW - A solemn promise made to God freely and deliberately to perform some good work or to embrace a higher state of life.

-W-

WARDEN - (Sl. Starosta) A lay officer presiding over the church council, elected at a parish meeting.

Weekly Cycle. Each day of the Week is dedicated to certain special commemorations: Sunday - Christ's Resurrection; Monday - Holy Bodiless Powers (Angels); Tuesday - the prophets and St. John the Forerunner and Baptist of the Lord; Wednesday - Cross and recalls Judas' betrayal; Thursday – The Holy Apostles and Hierarchs; Friday - The Cross and recalls the day of the Crucifixion; Saturday - All Saints, especially the Mother of God, and to the memory of all those who have departed this life in the hope of resurrection and eternal life.

WESTERN CHURCH -The part of the Universal Church which separated in 1054 with the Pope of Rome at the head. Commonly referred to as the Roman Catholic Church.

WESTERN RITE. Those Orthodox that follow a Rite with forms that developed in the west before the separation of Rome from the Orthodox Church. This is a small group approved for use in only two jurisdictions.

WITNESS - (Gr. martyria) 1) One who testifies by word and deed. In the New Testament, the word is also rendered "martyr," a reference to those who give their lives for the gospel of Christ. Also, the Holy Spirit bears witness to the spirits of those who believe in Christ, that they belong to

Him. (Rom. 8:16; Heb. 10:15; 12:1; 1 John 5:6 12; Rev. 11:3 12.) See also MARTYR.

WONDERWORKER - (1) Generally speaking, a wonderworker (also called "miracle-worker") is someone who is known for miracles God, the source of all miracles and wonders, has worked through them. (2) One of the various customary saint titles used to in commemoration at divine services when remembering saints on the Church Calendar.

WORSHIP is to render praise, glory, and thanksgiving to God: the Father, the Son, and the Holy Spirit. All humanity is called to worship God. Worship is more than being in the "great-out-of-doors", or listening to a sermon, or singing a hymn. God can be known in His creation, but that doesn't constitute worship. And as helpful as sermons may be, they can never offer a proper substitute for worship. Most prominent in Orthodox worship is the corporate praise, thanksgiving, and glory given to God by the Church. This worship is consummated in intimate communion with God at His Holy Table.

WORTHY - (Gr. axios) Describes those who act in a manner befitting one who is a follower of Christ. No one is worthy of salvation in and of himself, but all are made worthy through Christ (1 Thess. 2:10-12). see AXIOS

-X-

XEROPHAGY - (literally, "dry eating") Vegetables cooked with water and salt (no oil), or uncooked dry food.

-Y-

Year of the Church. (see calendar).

Ypakoe. This is a short Troparion sung at Matins on Great Feasts and Sundays.

-Z-

Zapivka ("washing down") is the liturgical practice in the Orthodox Church, primarily within that of the Slavic tradition, whereby the faithful will partake of antidoron (blessed bread) and some wine diluted with warm water after receiving Holy Communion.

Zeon. (Gr. "boiling"). The hot water used by the priest for the Eucharist. It is added to the chalice during the Communion hymn in commemoration of the water that flowed out of the side of the crucified Christ when he was pierced with the spear.

ZEAL - Devotion; enthusiastic obedience to God; a quality of divine diligence or fervor. Christians are called to follow Christ with enthusiasm and zeal (Acts 18:25; Rom. 12:10, 11) and - warned against misguided enthusiasm, a zeal "not according to knowledge" (Rom. 10:2).

ZEON - (Gr. boiling). The hot water used by the priest for the Eucharist. It is added to the chalice during the Communion hymn in commemoration of the water that flowed out of the side of the crucified Christ when he was pierced with the spear.

ZHERTVENNIK - (Sl.) The Table of Oblation which is against the left wall of the Sanctuary. Here the Proskomedia (preparation of the holy elements) is made before the beginning of the Divine Liturgy. The elements remain on the Zhertvennik until the Great Entrance, when they are taken by the priest through the Royal doors and placed upon the altar.

Zone. The belt or girdle worn by the priests on his *stichar*. It signifies the power of faith.

www.ingramcontent.com/pod-product-compliance
Lightning Source LLC
Chambersburg PA
CBHW061818250726
48657CB00001B/477